The Author

LENNARTH PETERSSON is a modelmaker and draughtsman who has spent many years studying eighteenth-century rigs and rigging. He has written for journals and periodicals and, amongst many commissions, has produced detailed visual interpretations of the *Vasa* for the Statens Sjohistoriska Museet in Stockholm. He lives in Sweden. His companion volume, *Rigging Period Ship Models*, is also published by Seaforth Publishing.

RIGGING
PERIOD FORE-AND-AFT CRAFT

LENNARTH PETERSSON

Seaforth
PUBLISHING

To Eva

Copyright © Lennarth Petersson 2007

This paperback edition first published in Great Britain in 2015 by
Seaforth Publishing,
Pen & Sword Books Ltd,
47 Church Street,
Barnsley S70 2AS

www.seaforthpublishing.com

First published in 2007 by Chatham Publishing

British Library Cataloguing in Publication Data
A catalogue record for this book is available from the British Library

ISBN 978 1 84832 218 9

Typeset and designed by Roger Daniels
Printed and bound in China by 1010 Printing International Ltd

Contents

Introduction • 7
Acknowledgements • 9

THE BRITISH NAVAL CUTTER • 10
Profile & Deck Plan • 12
Belaying Plan • 14
Channels • 16
Shrouds • 17
Toprope • 18
Topmast Shrouds • 19
Forestay • 20
Backstay • 22
Bowsprit Guys • 23
Jib Outhaul & Inhaul • 24
Jib Halliard • 25
Lower yard Sling • 26
Topsail Yard Halliard • 27
Lifts • 28
Cluelines & Sheets • 29
Lower Yard Braces &
    Topsail Yard Braces • 30
Throat Halliard • 32
Peak Halliard • 33
Topping Lift • 34
Mainsheet • 35
Jib • 36
Foresail • 37
Pendant & Flag Hoists • 38

THE FRENCH LUGGER • 40
Profile & Deck Plan • 42
Deck & Rail Details • 44
Belaying Plan • 46
Fore, Main & Mizzen Channels • 48
Fore Shrouds • 49
Main Shrouds & Tackle • 50
Mainstay • 51
Mizzenstay • 52
Bobstay & Bowsprit Shrouds • 53
Jib • 54
Foresail Yard • 55
Foresail • 56
Fore Topsail • 57
Mainsail Yard • 58
Mainsail • 59
Main Topsail • 60
Mizzen Yard & Sail • 61
Bumpkin • 62
Mizzen Topsail • 63
Anchor Gear • 64

THE AMERICAN SCHOONER • 66
Profile & Deck Plan • 68
Belaying Plan • 70
Fore Channels • 72
Main Channels • 73
Fore tackle & Top • 74
Main Tackle & Top • 75
Fore Shrouds & Deadeyes • 76
Main Shrouds & Deadeyes • 77
Toprope • 78
Forestay • 79
Mainstay • 80
Fore Topmast &
    Topgallant Shrouds • 81
Main Topmast Shrouds • 82
Backstays • 83
Bobstay • 84
Bowsprit Guy, Martingale Stays,
    Jibboom Guys • 85
Jib Stays • 86
Flying Jib Stay • 87
Main Topmast & Topgallant Stay • 88
Foremast Yards • 89
Fore Yard Sling, Topsail & Topgallant
    Yard Halliards • 90
Lifts • 91
Braces • 92
Fore Throat & Peak Halliards • 94
Fore Vangs • 95
Main Throat & Peak Halliards,
    Main Vangs • 96
Main Boom Topping Lift • 97
Mainsheet & Steering Gear • 98
Mainsail Outhaul • 99
Flying Jib • 100
Jib • 101
Fore Staysail • 102
Fore Course Clueline,
    Buntline & Sheet • 103
Fore Course Bowlines • 104
Fore Topsail Clueline & Reef Tackle • 105
Fore Topsail Sheet, Bowline &
    Buntline • 106
Fore Topgallant Clueline,
    Bowline & Sheet • 107
Fore Gaff Sail • 108
Main Gaff Topsail, Swedish Fashion • 109
Main Gaff Topsail, American
    Fashion • 110
Mainsail • 111

A fleet of fore-and-afters at anchor has its own slender graciousness. The setting of their sails resembles more than anything else the unfolding of a bird's wings; the facility of their evolutions is a pleasure to the eye. They are birds of the sea, whose swimming is like flying, and resembles more a natural function than the handling of man-invented appliances. The fore- and-aft rig in its simplicity and the beauty of its aspect under every angle of vision is, I believe, unapproachable. A schooner, yawl, or cutter in charge of a capable man seems to handle herself as if endowed with the power of reasoning and the gift of swift execution. One laughs with sheer pleasure at a smart piece of manoeuvring, as at a manifestation of a living creature's quick wit and graceful precision.

JOSEPH CONRAD
The Mirror of the Sea

Introduction

As a professional illustrator and an amateur model-maker I have, along with many others, often found it so difficult to find detailed information about ships and vessels that I have wanted to depict or replicate. This is particularly true when it comes to the rigging of ships, and particularly the rigs of smaller craft. My first book, *Rigging Period Ship Models*, was intended to help modellers, and anyone with an interest in the ships of that period, understand the three-masted ship rig. The enthusiasm with which that book seems to have been received suggested that I should try and do the same for the smaller, fore-and-aft rigged craft.

After searching for suitable prototypes with assistance of the publisher, I finally alighted on three different models representing vessels of a moderate size. These are an American schooner, a British naval cutter and a French lugger.

Ship models are fascinating objects to study, and it is easy to be drawn into a world of fantasy onboard, but it was important to stick to the task I was pursuing and the more I became acquainted with the ships, the more I have realised the limits of my own knowledge. I have, as in my previous book, attempted to describe and illustrate no more than the rigs of these vessels. Readers wanting more information on the design, construction and careers of these sorts of craft will need to look elsewhere.

The model of the American-built schooner *Experiment* was made in Sweden some time after she was bought into the Swedish Royal Navy in 1812, and it differs somewhat from the drawings published by Howard Chapelle in his *The Search for Speed under Sail*. The model does not carry any sails but I have made an attempt at reconstructing them, with the exception of the middle staysail, not having found any reliable representation of such a sail. I also show two versions of the main topsail, as the model does not carry any spar indicating which kind of sail was used.

Drawings preserved in the War Archives in Stockholm of *Falk* and *L' Áigle*, both of which were built on the lines of the *Experiment*, show different versions.

Likewise, the model of the naval cutter does not carry any sails and I have chosen to show only the jib and the foresail. Nevertheless, I hope the reader will be able to deduce and reconstruct the topsail and the mainsail from all the other drawings depicting the spars and the running rigging which are to be seen in the original model.

The French lugger is the most complete model and perhaps the most suitable to replicate with sails. The rig of the model is straightforward and functional, and is also the one that seems to have been least intervened with over the years.

The book is not intended to be an academic contribution to the field of maritime historical research; as a visual study based solely on three models it is rather intended as an accessible guide for the enthusiast and model shipwright. These contemporary models were all made by people well acquainted with the vessels of the period, and so they can be seen as representing some of the best evidence of the way these craft were rigged. Furthermore, there is a real advantage in being able to walk around a three-dimensional model as opposed to looking at a two-dimensional painting; I hope I have been able to bring some of that three-dimensional vision onto the printed page.

It has been exciting to be allowed the opportunity to analyse these models and I hope that the illustrations will be an inspiration to other modelmakers. Personally, I cannot imagine a more beautiful ornament in a home than a ship model, regardless of whether it is made by an ambitious and careful enthusiast or by a professional with a fancy for the sea.

LENNARTH PETERSSON
Habo, February 2007

Acknowledgements

The names of the makers of the models are sadly lost in the mists of time, as is so often the case. Fortunately, their skilled work has survived to tell us a story, but without the aid of many persons of great knowledge and learning it would have been very hard for me to create the drawings found in this book.

I am in particular very grateful for the friendship of Manne Dunge, Tom Ohlsson and Per-Inge Lindqvist of the Marinmuseet in Karlskrona, Sweden, and for their help generously given; also for the assistance given me by Peter Fitzgerald of the Science Museum in London and Bernard Bryant of the National Maritime Museum in Greenwich, as well as from Olof Pipping in Alingsås, Sweden. Without the generous assistance and patience, as always, of Julian Mannering of Chatham Publishing this book would not have been launched at all.

The British
Naval
Cutter

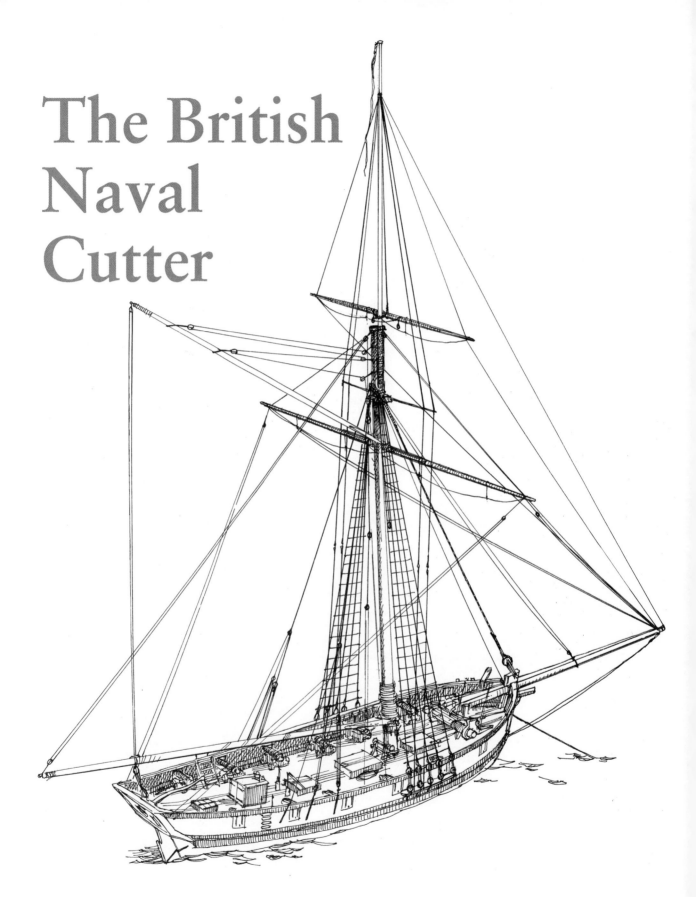

THE FOLLOWING DRAWINGS, portraying the rigging of an eighteenth-century naval cutter, are based upon a rigged model in the Science Museum in London. This model represents one of the larger naval cutters that were built in the second half of the eighteenth century to counter the ever-increasing smuggling trade. It has been estimated that at one point in the mid-eighteenth century there were some twenty thousand professional smugglers at work but only a pitiful collection of thirty revenue boats, small King's ships and under-rigged revenue sloops, to police the entire British coastline. A Parliamentary committee was formed in 1745 to look into 'the most infamous practice of smuggling and consider the most effective methods to prevent the said practice.' A new generation of revenue cutter emerged after the Seven Years War, developed by the Navy, and these were evolved from the fast trading craft that had been used in the Channel in the previous decades for both legal and illicit trade. The naval cutters were clinker-built vessels with a broad beam and bluff bows, though fine lined beneath the waterline, and they had a deep draft and low freeboard; in their role patrolling the Channel they were designed to remain at sea in most weathers. To give them the sort of speed that was required a massive sail area was piled on to drive the hull through the water and carry the added weight of, in this case, twelve guns, two carronades and twelve swivels.

Falconer, in his *Universal Dictionary of the Marine*, gives as clear a definition of a cutter of this period as any describing it as 'a small vessel commonly navigated in the Channel of England, furnished with one mast and a straight-running bowsprit that can be run in on the deck occasionally; except which, and the largeness of the sails, that are rigged much like sloops. Many of these vessels are used on an illicit trade, and others employed by the Government to seize them, the latter of which are either under the direction of the Admiralty or Custom-house'.

A quick glance at the spars of this vessel confirms the huge sail area. The mast, gaff and boom are all long and the topmast seems almost excessively so; the five shrouds on each side would have been needed to carry the colossal weight of sail and, unlike a sloop, the forestay led to the stem, not to the end of the bowsprit. This horizontal running spar is likewise huge and at its end carried the topmast stay. A square topsail was carried while the spar for a square-sail on the mast is shown just above the deck.

The dimensions measured from the 1:30 scale model are: length of gundeck 69ft, length of keel 49ft, beam 24ft and depth of hold 11ft. The hull of this model is contemporary and its dimensions conform closely to the draught of the *Expedition*, a cutter designed by Sir J Williams and built at Dover in 1778. This draught is held in the draught collection at the National Maritime Museum where there can also be seen a model of the cutter *Hawke*, dated 1777, which offers the rare sight of a full suit of sails.

These heavily-sparred cutters were amongst the fastest vessels of their day and they came to acquire other roles in the Navy. Their speed made them fine dispatch craft and their up-wind abilities recommended them for reconnaissance in those waters where the less handy square-rigged vessel found it difficult manoeuvre.

Profile & Deck Plan

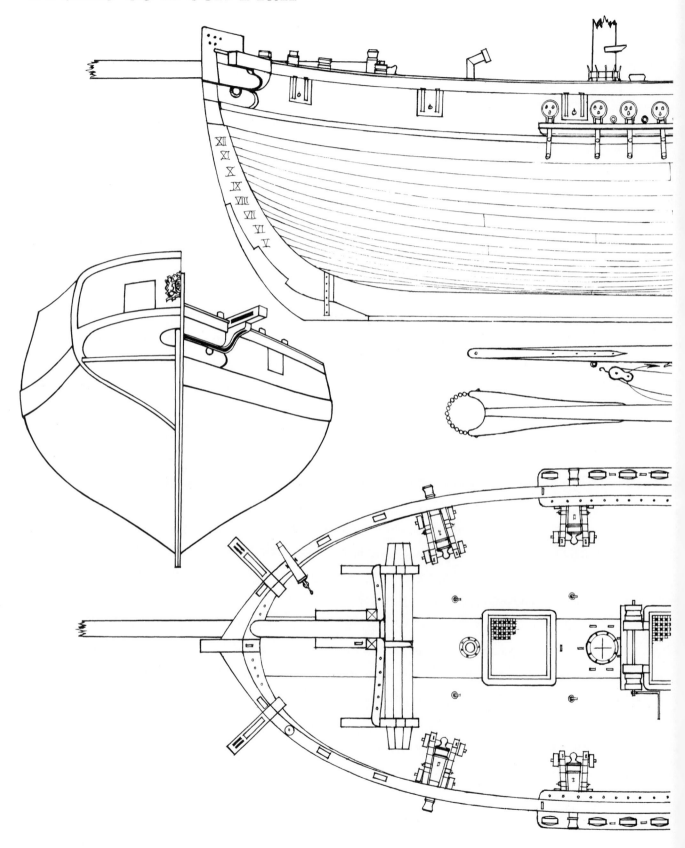

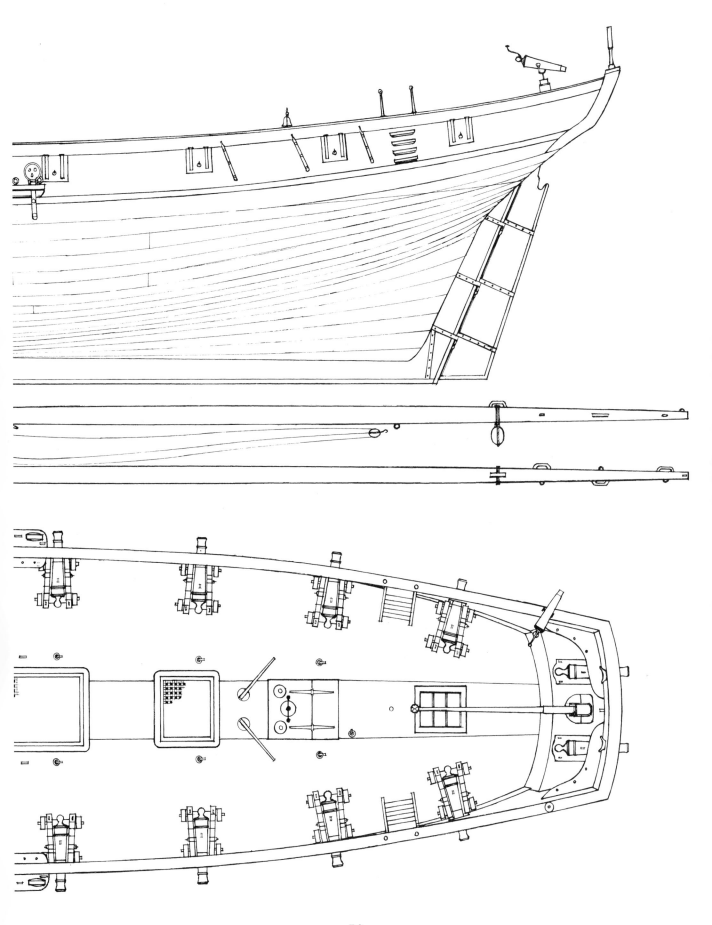

Belaying Plan

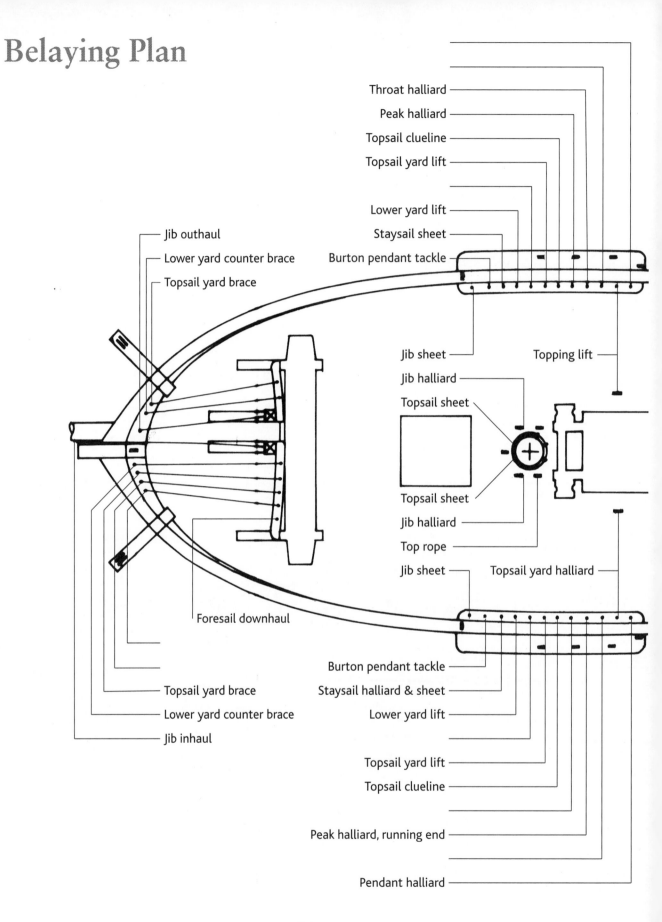

Throat halliard

Peak halliard

Topsail clueline

Topsail yard lift

Lower yard lift

Staysail sheet

Burton pendant tackle

Jib outhaul

Lower yard counter brace

Topsail yard brace

Jib sheet

Topping lift

Jib halliard

Topsail sheet

Topsail sheet

Jib halliard

Top rope

Jib sheet

Topsail yard halliard

Foresail downhaul

Topsail yard brace

Lower yard counter brace

Jib inhaul

Burton pendant tackle

Staysail halliard & sheet

Lower yard lift

Topsail yard lift

Topsail clueline

Peak halliard, running end

Pendant halliard

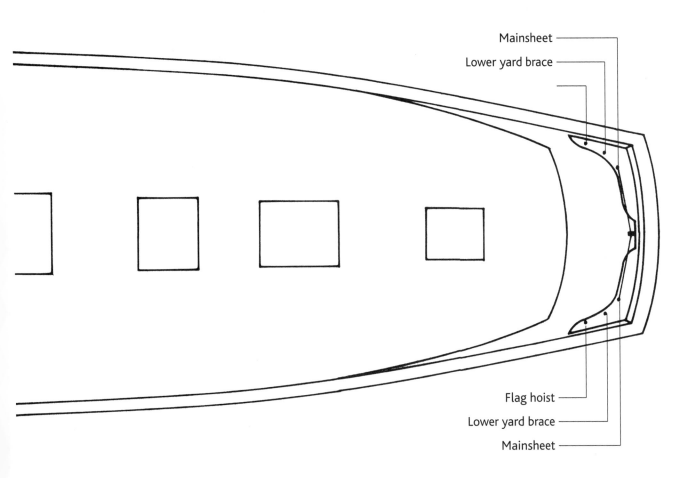

Mainsheet

Lower yard brace

Flag hoist

Lower yard brace

Mainsheet

Channels

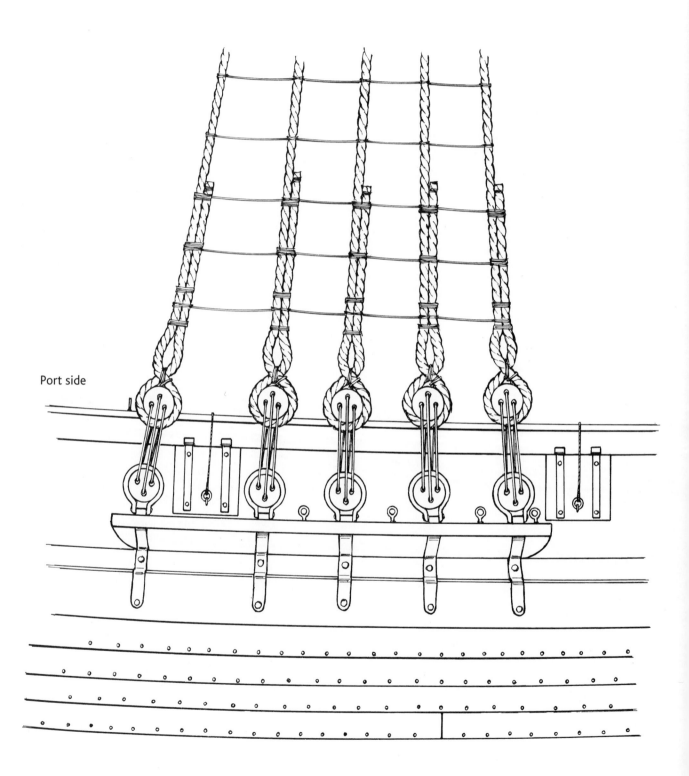

Port side

Shrouds

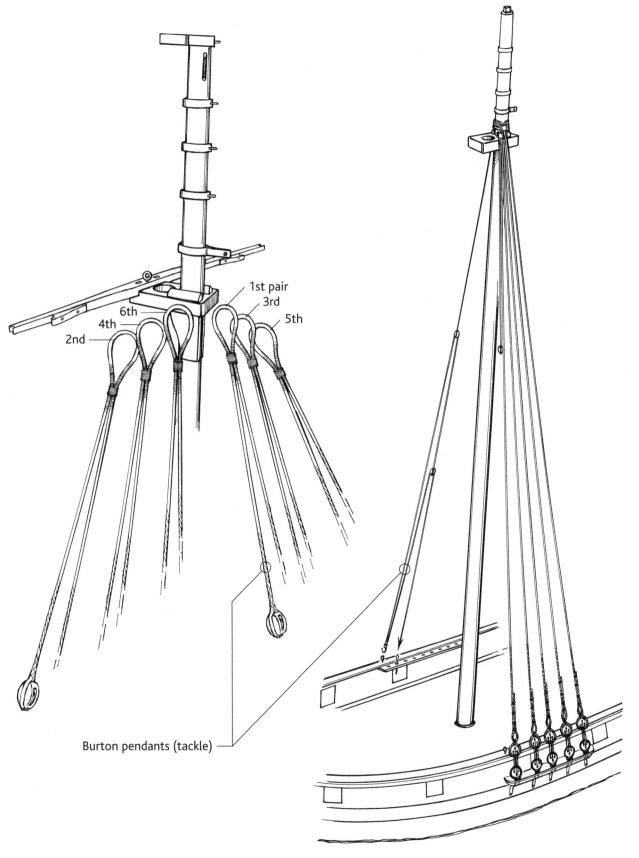

1st pair
3rd
6th
5th
4th
2nd

Burton pendants (tackle)

Toprope

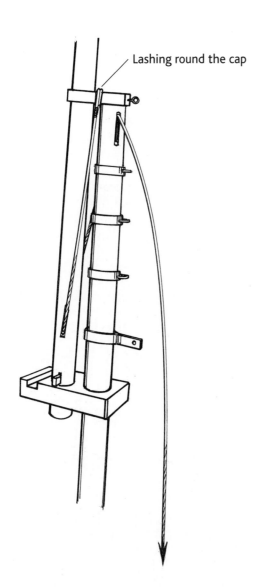

Lashing round the cap

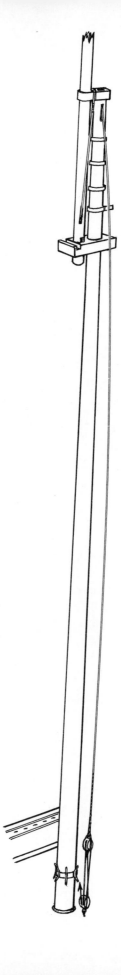

Topmast Shrouds

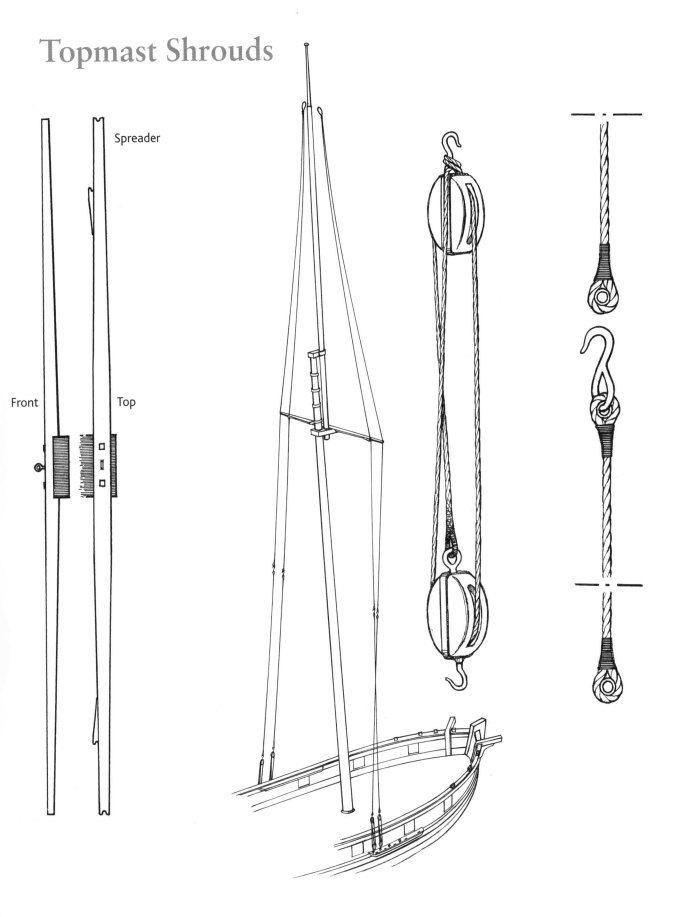

Spreader

Front   Top

Forestay

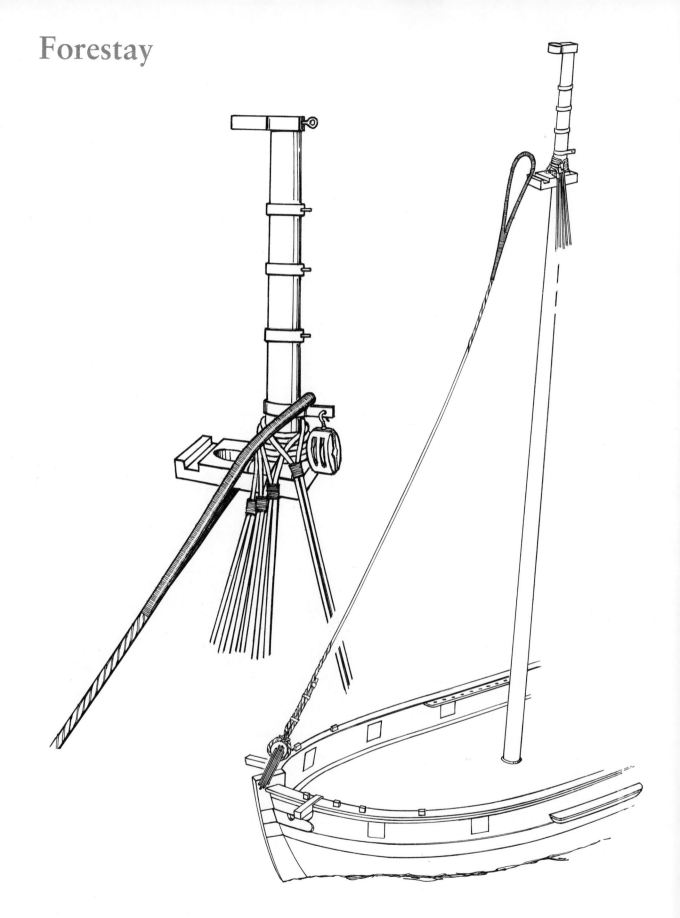

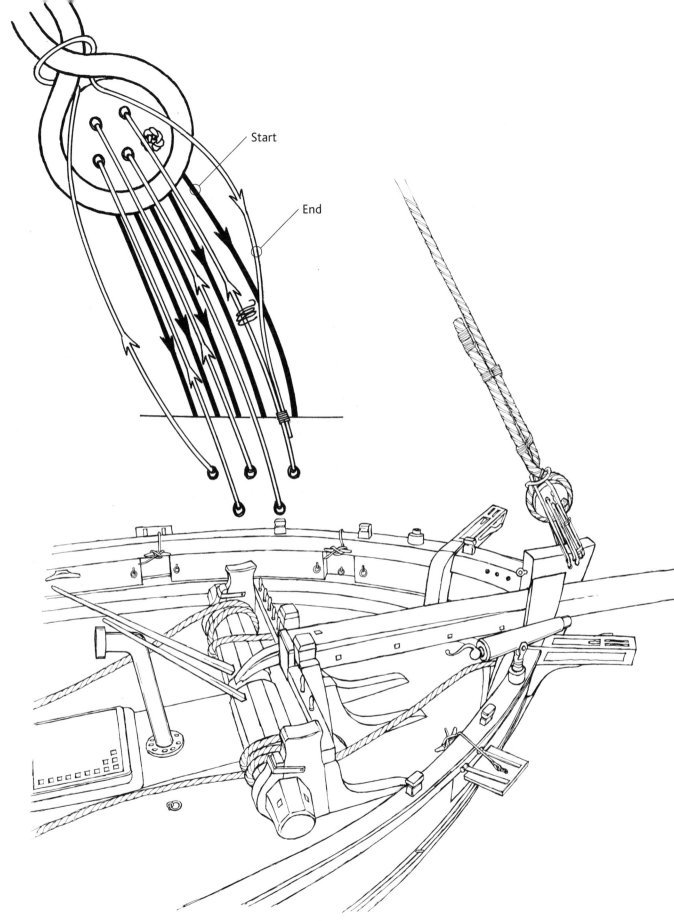

Start

End

Backstay

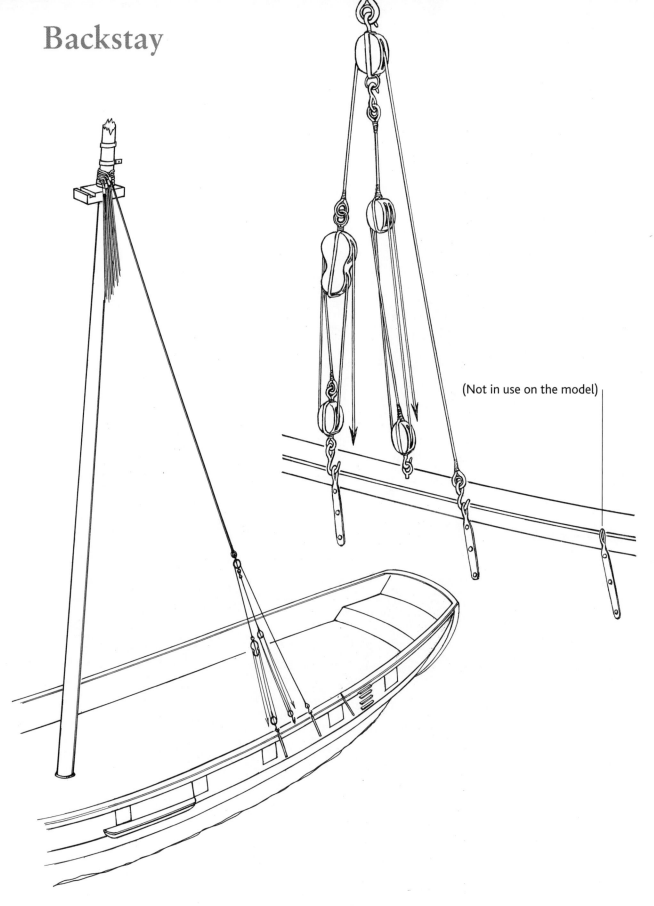

(Not in use on the model)

Bowsprit Guys

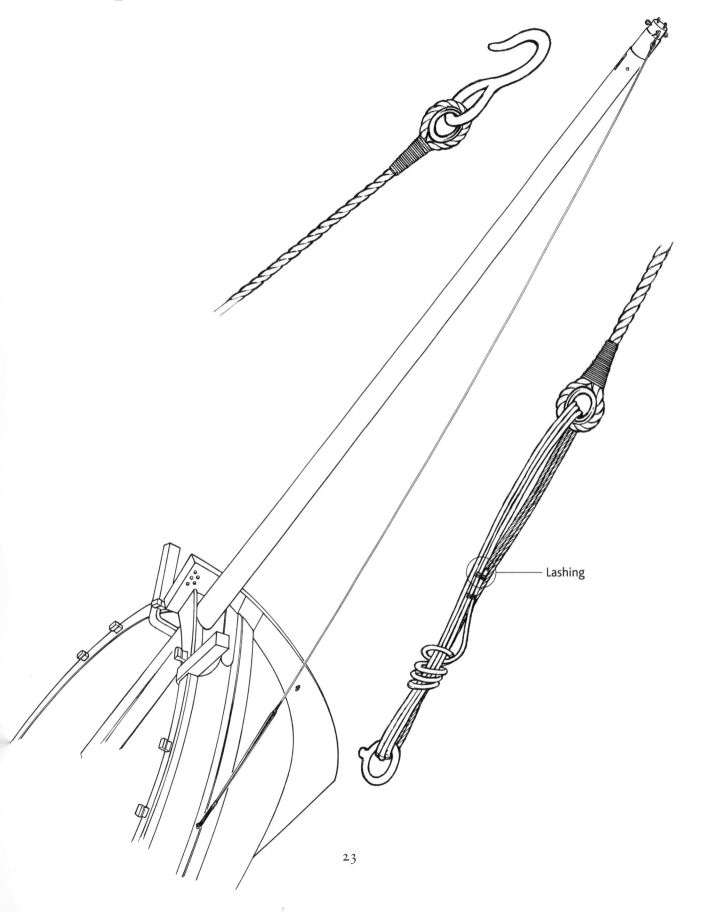

Lashing

Jib Outhaul & Inhaul

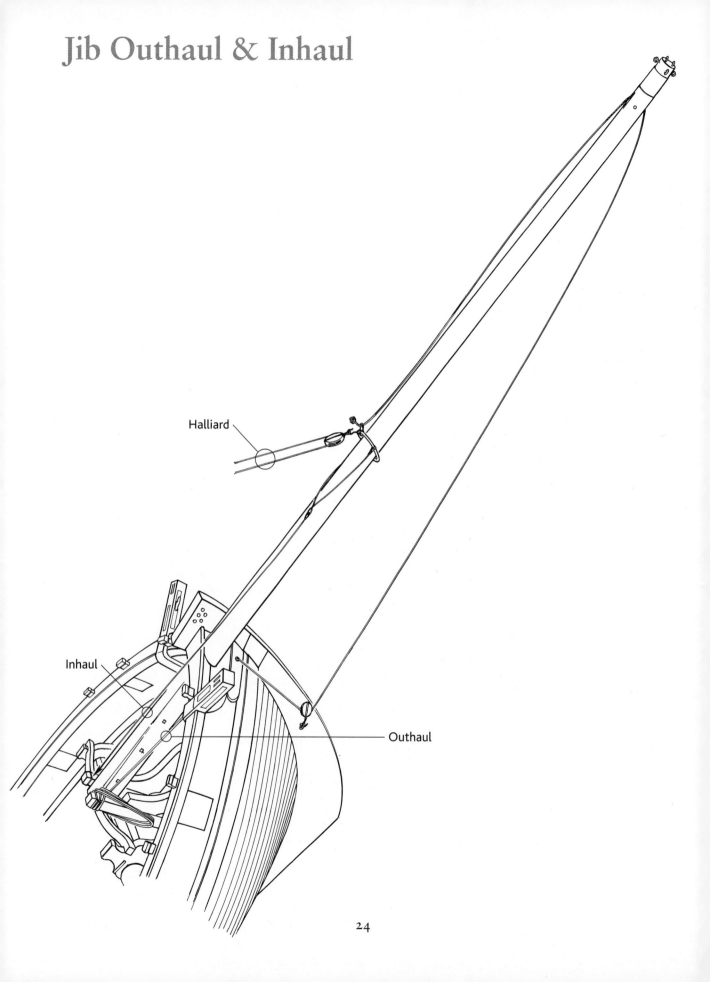

Halliard

Inhaul

Outhaul

Jib Halliard

Blocks lashed to the stay

Halliard

Inhaul

Outhaul

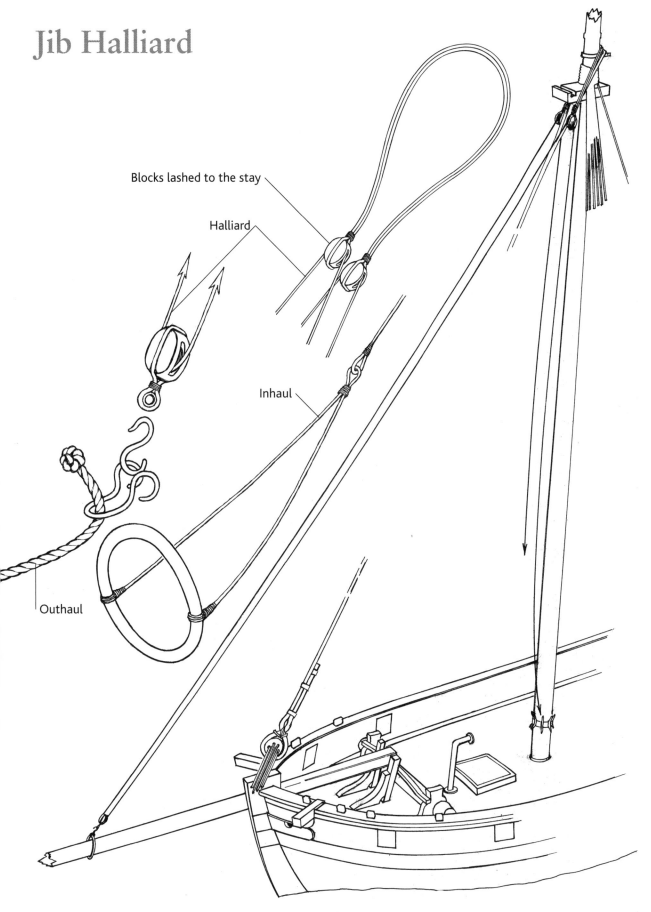

25

Lower Yard Sling

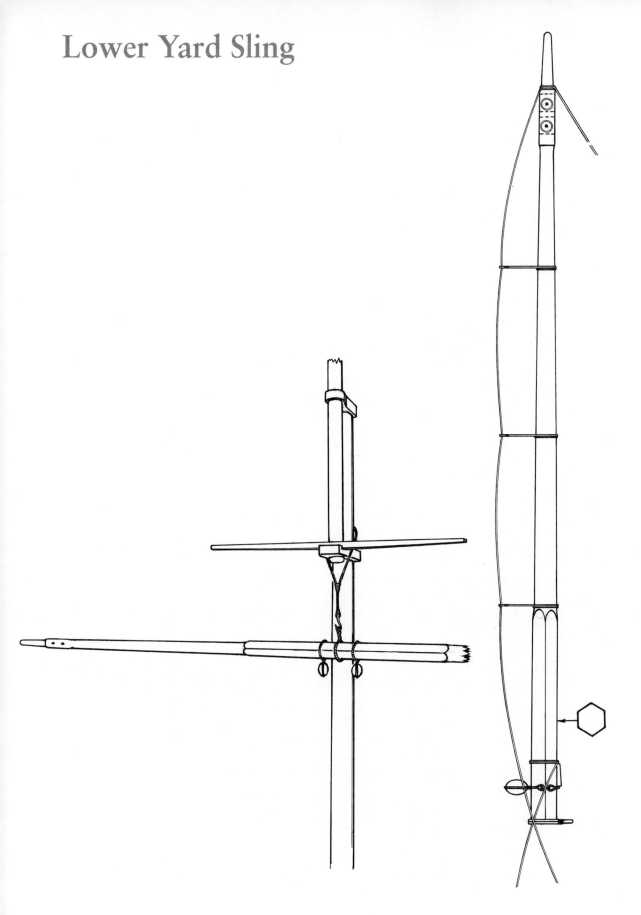

Topsail Yard Halliard

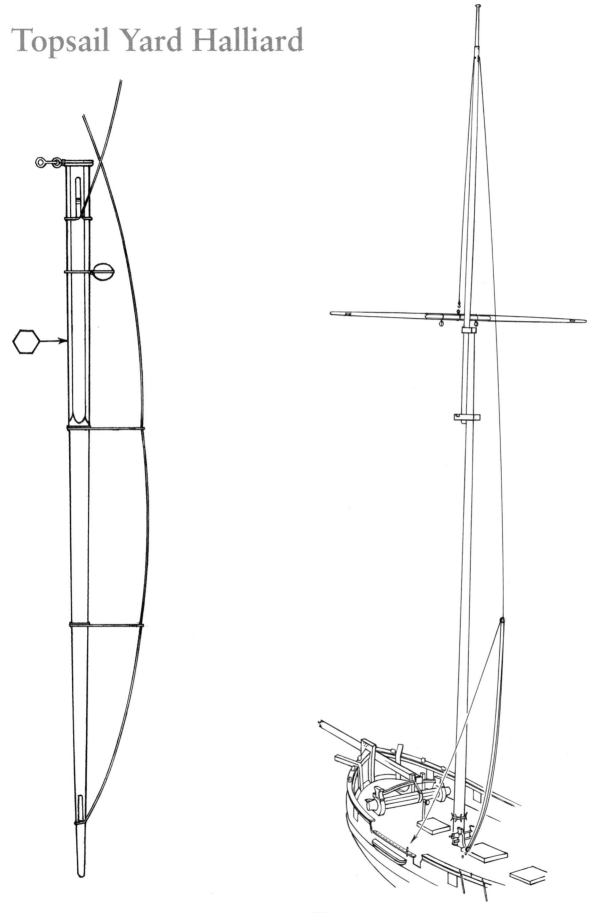

Lifts

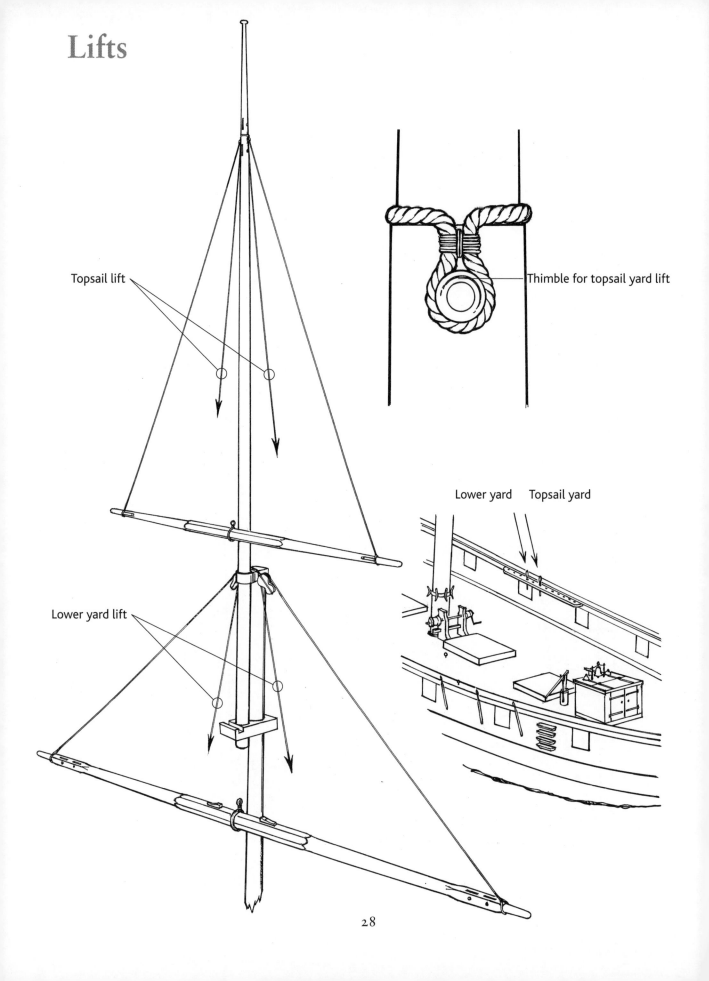

Topsail lift

Thimble for topsail yard lift

Lower yard lift

Lower yard   Topsail yard

Cluelines & Sheets

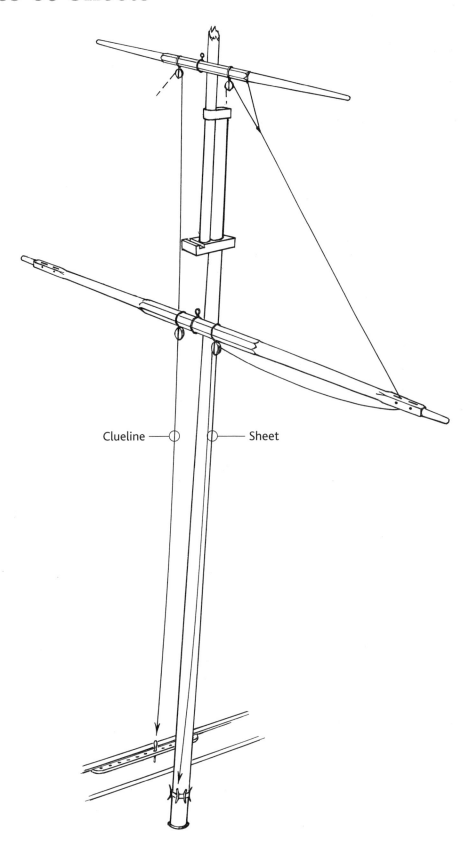

Clueline ───○   ○─── Sheet

Lower Yard Braces

& Topsail Yard Braces

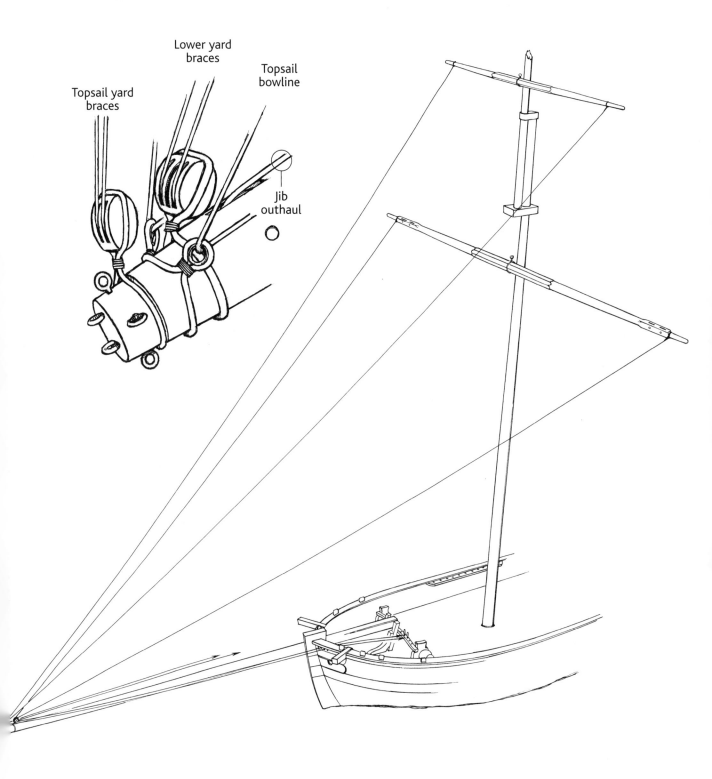

Topsail yard braces

Lower yard braces

Topsail bowline

Jib outhaul

Throat Halliard

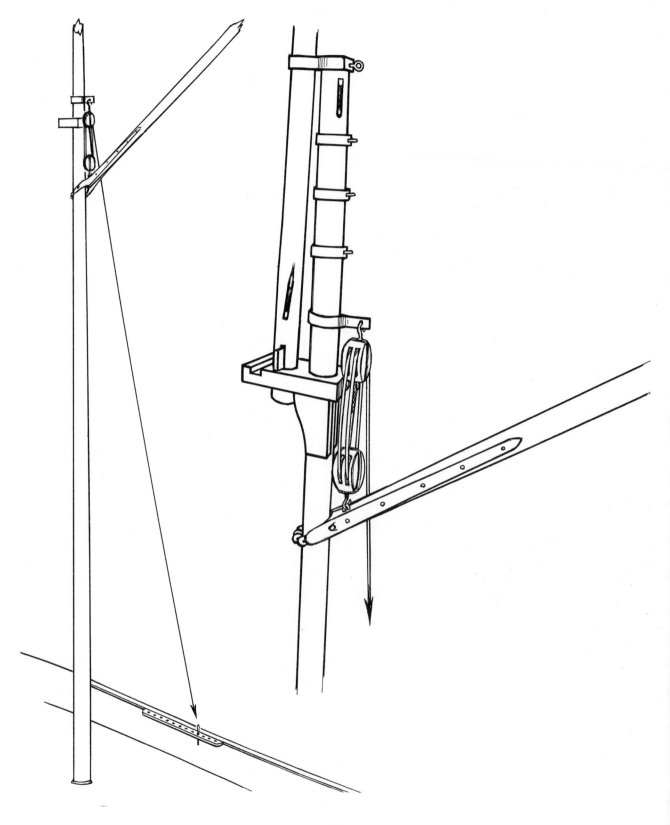

Peak Halliard

Topping Lift

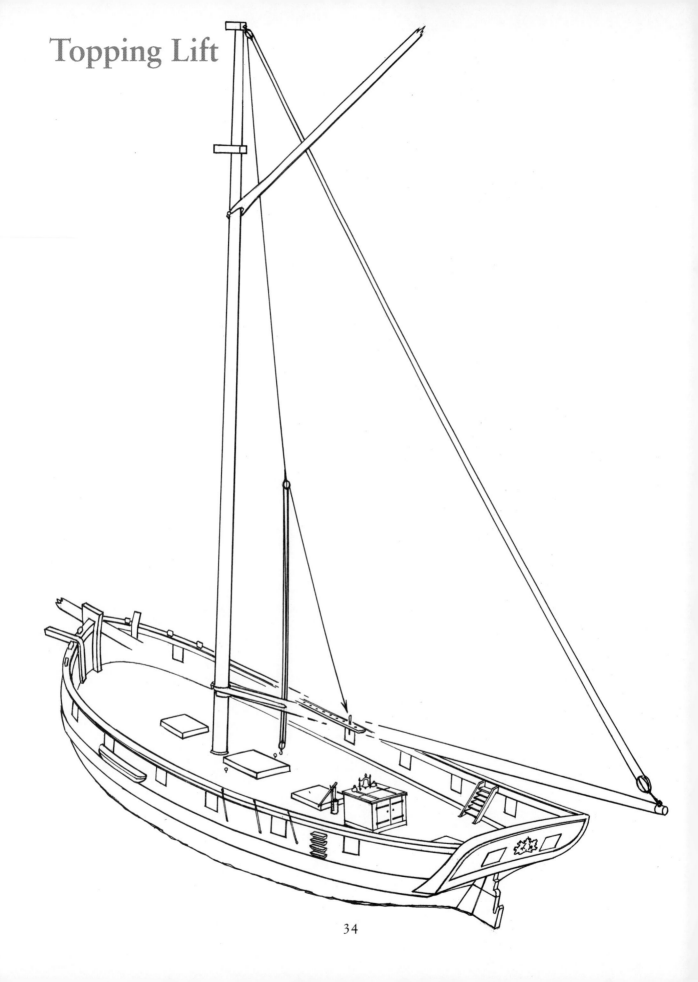

Mainsheet

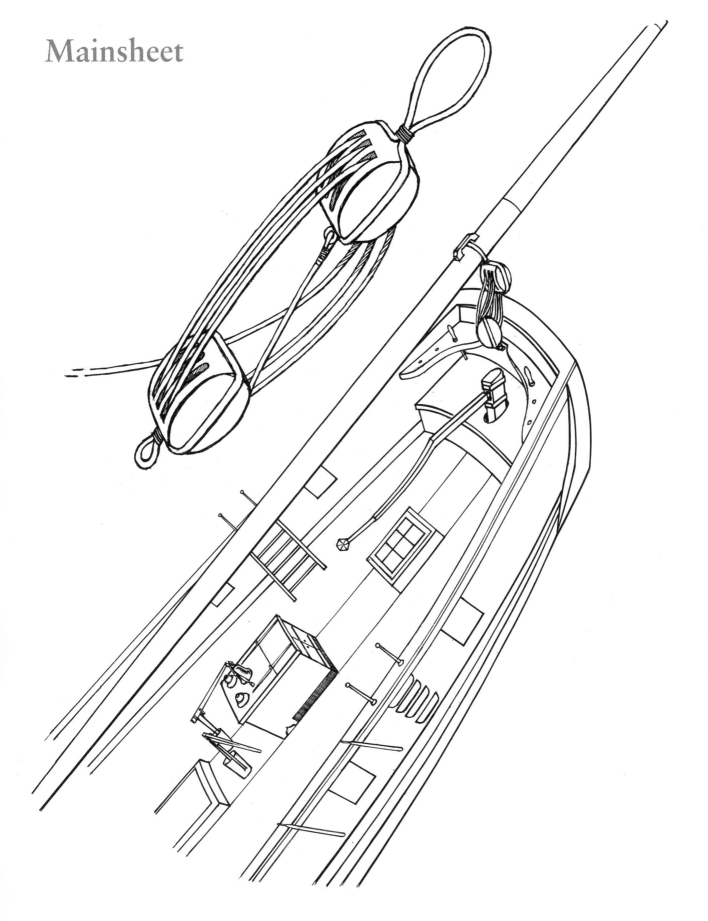

Jib

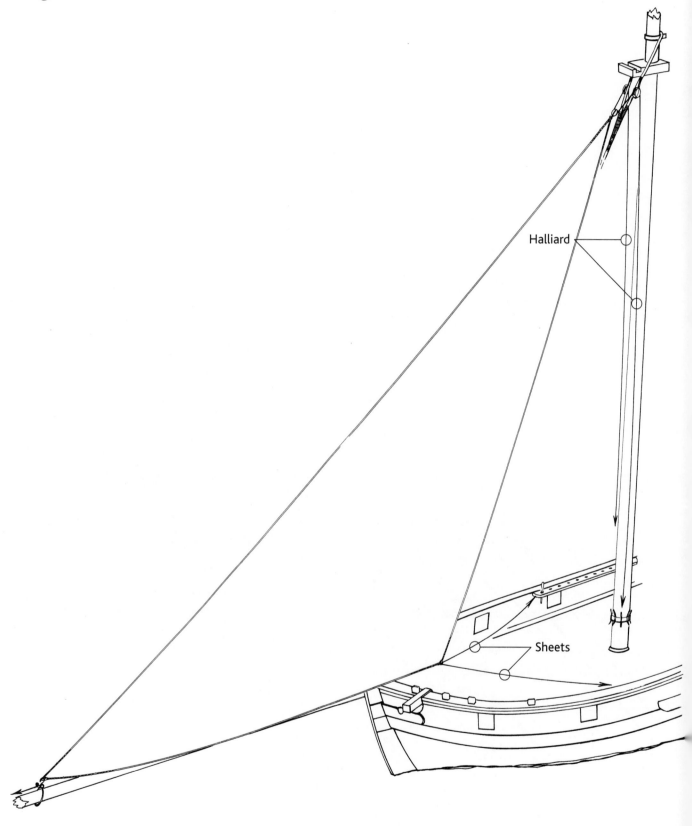

Halliard

Sheets

Foresail

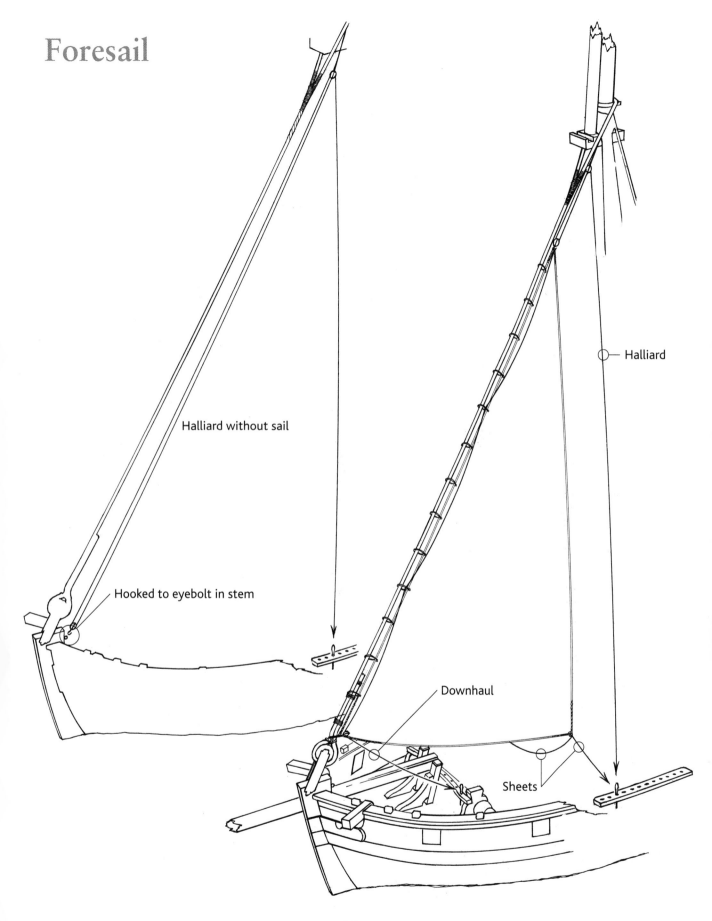

Halliard without sail

Hooked to eyebolt in stem

Halliard

Downhaul

Sheets

37

Pendant & Flag Hoists

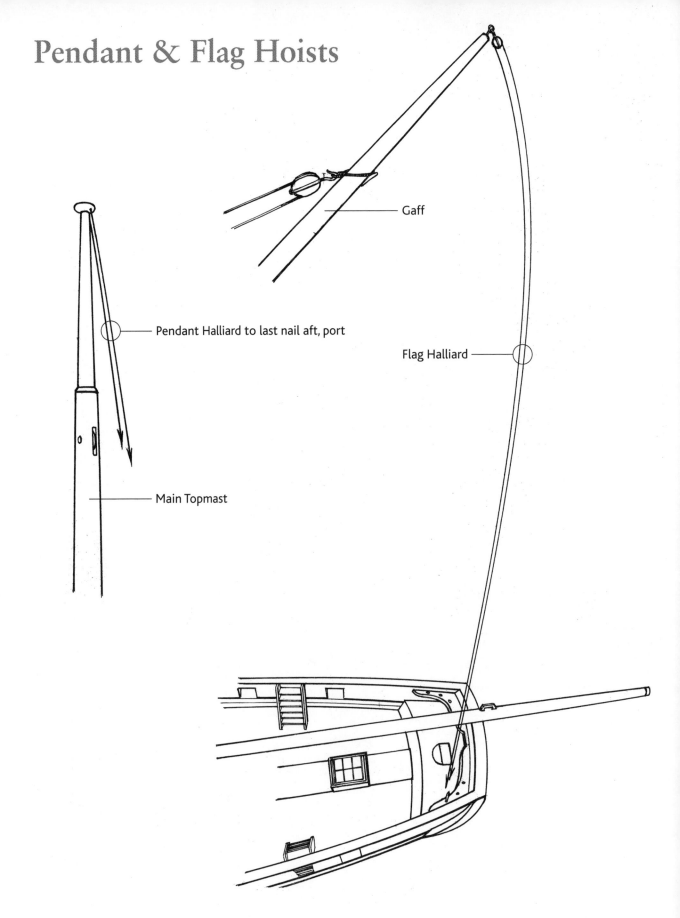

Gaff

Pendant Halliard to last nail aft, port

Flag Halliard

Main Topmast

The French Lugger

THE FRENCH LUGGER that is depicted on the following pages is a typical three-masted type that was used by the French privateers during the Napoleonic Wars, particularly in the English Channel where they harried and harassed British shipping. The corsairs, as privateers were known as in France, mostly operated out of Dunkirk and St Malo and were responsible for the capture of hundreds of British ships during the wars. Able to lie at sea, sometimes even with their gear down, perhaps in the lee of a headland, they would be practically invisible to a merchant ship making its way up or down Channel.

These armed luggers developed from the three-masted luggers that were used in the North Sea fisheries and the type survived through to the twentieth century in the form of the French chasse marée. They were fine-lined and light and very fast, particularly when hard on the wind – perhaps their fastest point of sailing – and it is, therefore, of little surprise that the type was also favoured by English smugglers who found it a weatherly contender to the British revenue cutter. With reduced resistance and turbulence from their minimal rigging they sailed in much cleaner air than the heavily-spared and rigged cutters and also pointed higher. The loose-footed sails were very powerful and these craft required large crews to sail them, but this was hardly a disadvantage to their employment as privateers where a large crew was required to fight.

The model at the National Maritime Museum is built to the scale of 1:24 and is dated around 1800. It is a contemporary full hull model, built plank on frame of clinker construction and it depicts a vessel with eight guns. The model is decked, equipped and fully rigged, with sails set, and both the rigging and the sails are original. At this scale the model represents a prototype of some 76ft length overall with a beam of 20ft and an approximate tonnage of 110 burden. One distinct characteristic can be seen in the stepping of the topmast abaft the mainmast; though the practice was very occasionally found on cutters it is generally a peculiarity of the big luggers of this period. Le Coureur was one such vessel, built by Denys of Dunkirk in 1776. She was captured by the Royal Navy cutter Alert on 17 June 1778 and there are both original plans of her as well as drawings made after her capture.

Profile & Deck Plan

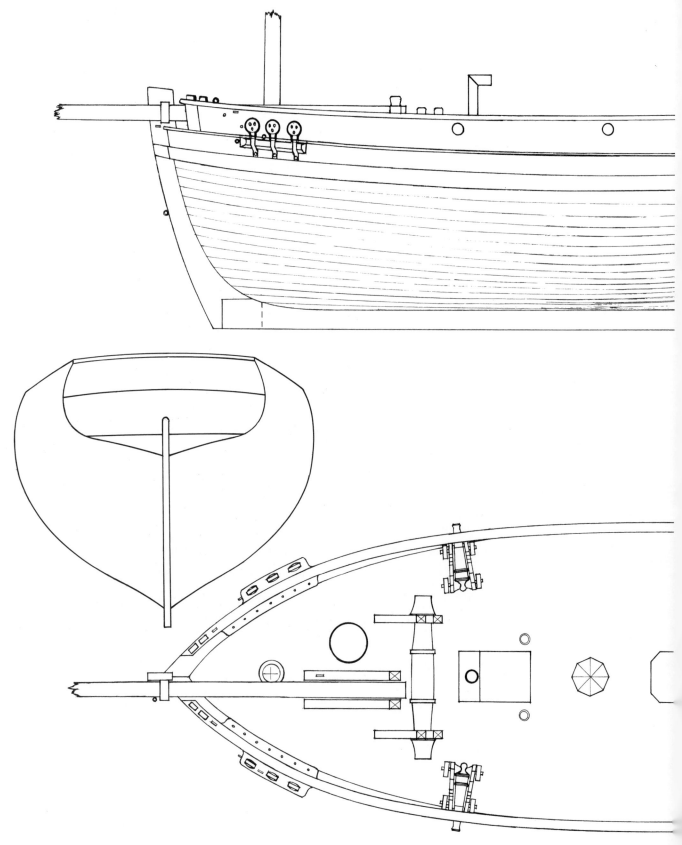

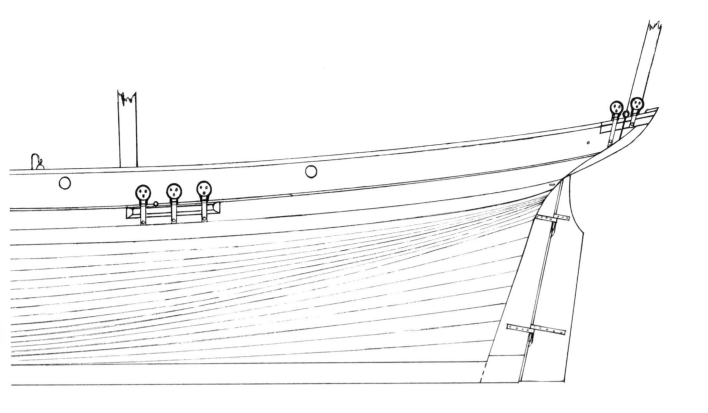

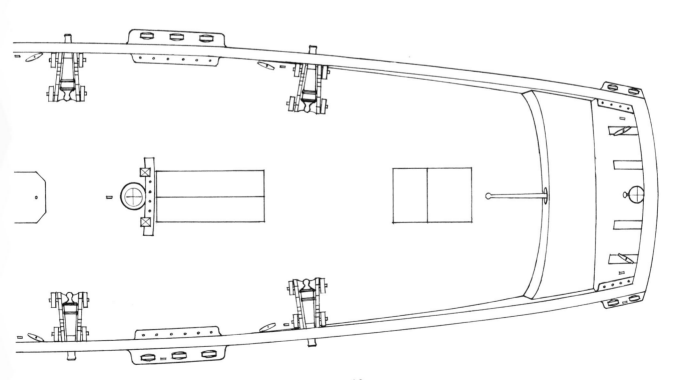

Deck & Rail details

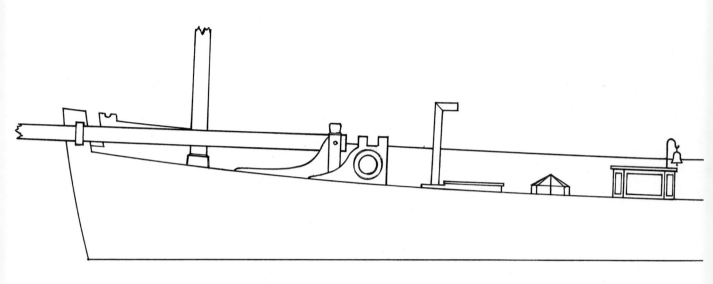

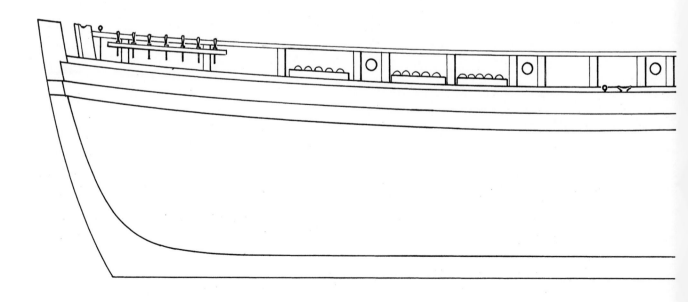

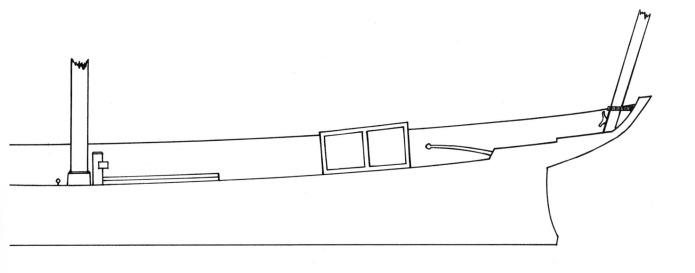

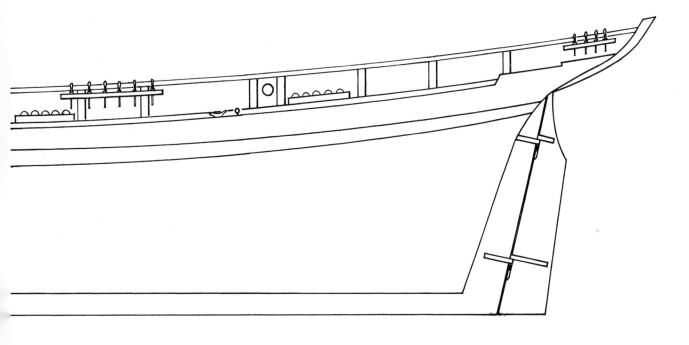

Belaying Plan

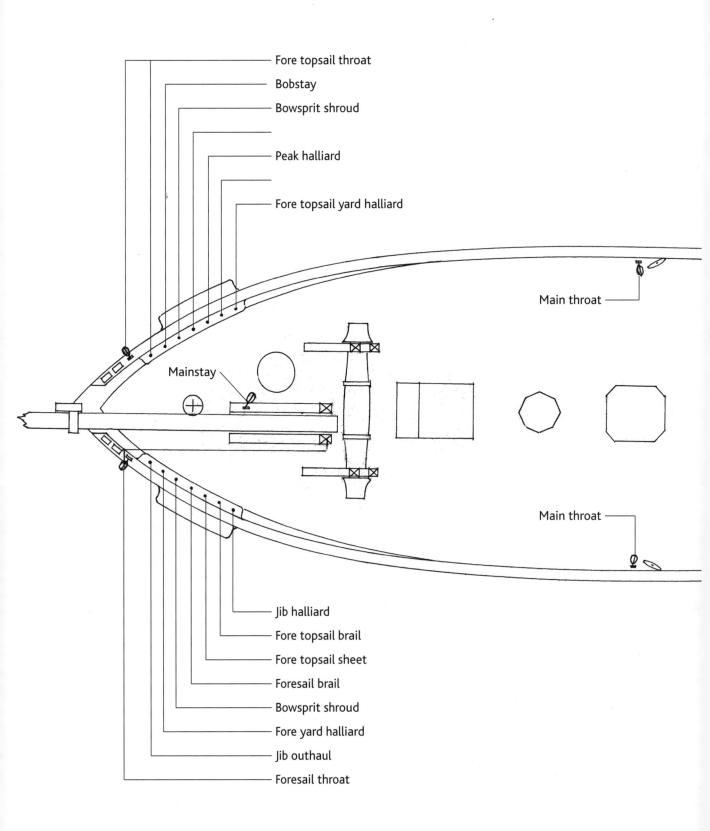

Fore topsail throat

Bobstay

Bowsprit shroud

Peak halliard

Fore topsail yard halliard

Main throat

Mainstay

Main throat

Jib halliard

Fore topsail brail

Fore topsail sheet

Foresail brail

Bowsprit shroud

Fore yard halliard

Jib outhaul

Foresail throat

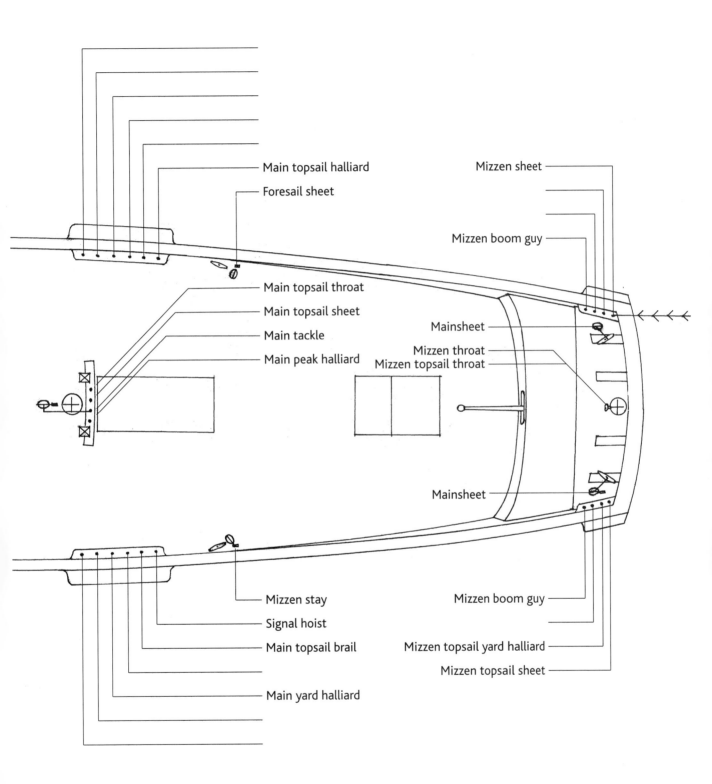

Main topsail halliard

Foresail sheet

Mizzen sheet

Mizzen boom guy

Main topsail throat

Main topsail sheet

Main tackle

Main peak halliard

Mainsheet

Mizzen throat

Mizzen topsail throat

Mainsheet

Mizzen stay

Signal hoist

Main topsail brail

Main yard halliard

Mizzen boom guy

Mizzen topsail yard halliard

Mizzen topsail sheet

Fore, Main, Mizzen Channels

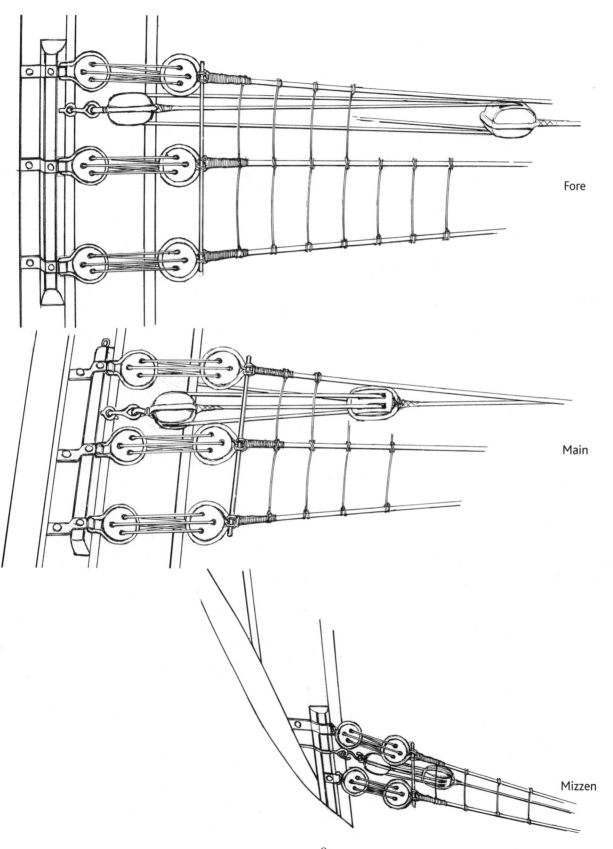

Fore

Main

Mizzen

Fore Shrouds

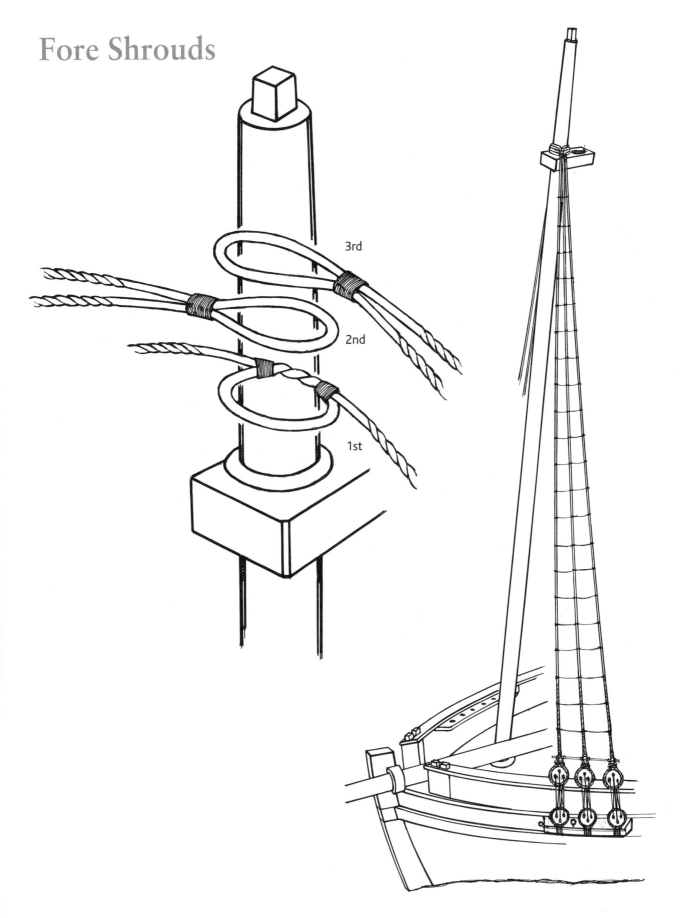

3rd

2nd

1st

Main Shrouds & Tackle

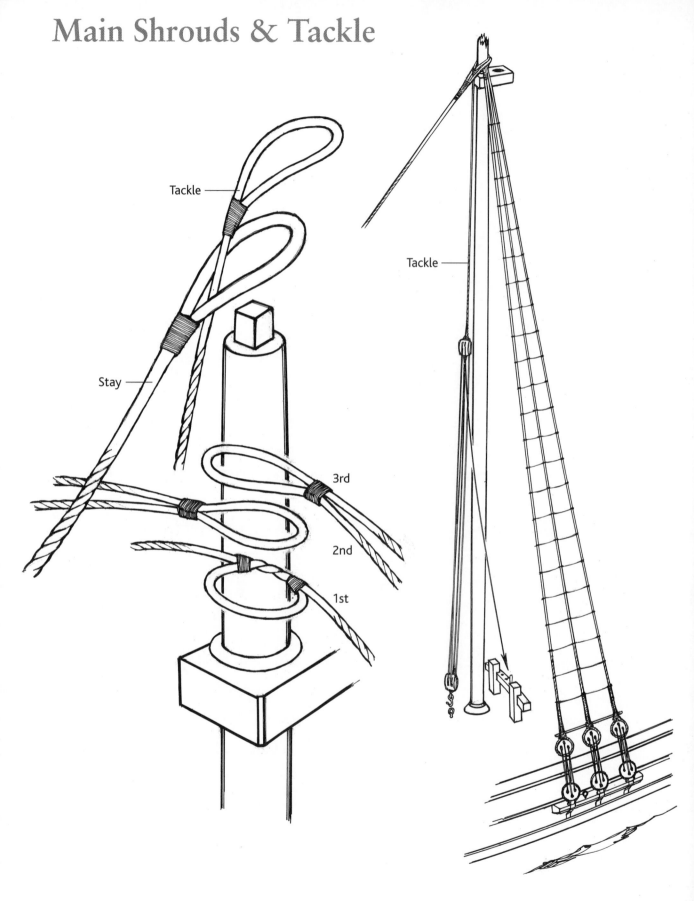

Tackle

Stay

Tackle

3rd

2nd

1st

Mainstay

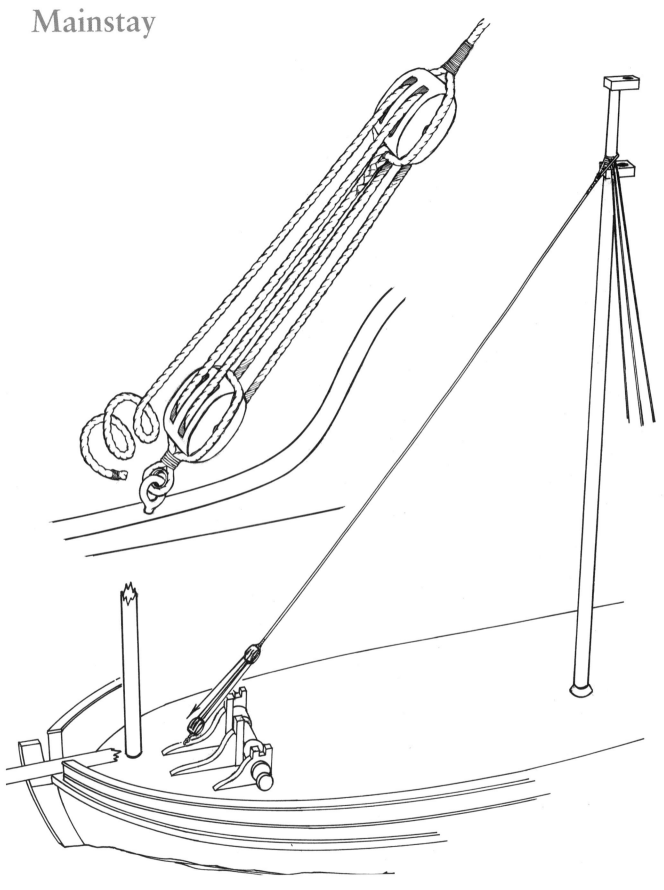

Mizzenstay

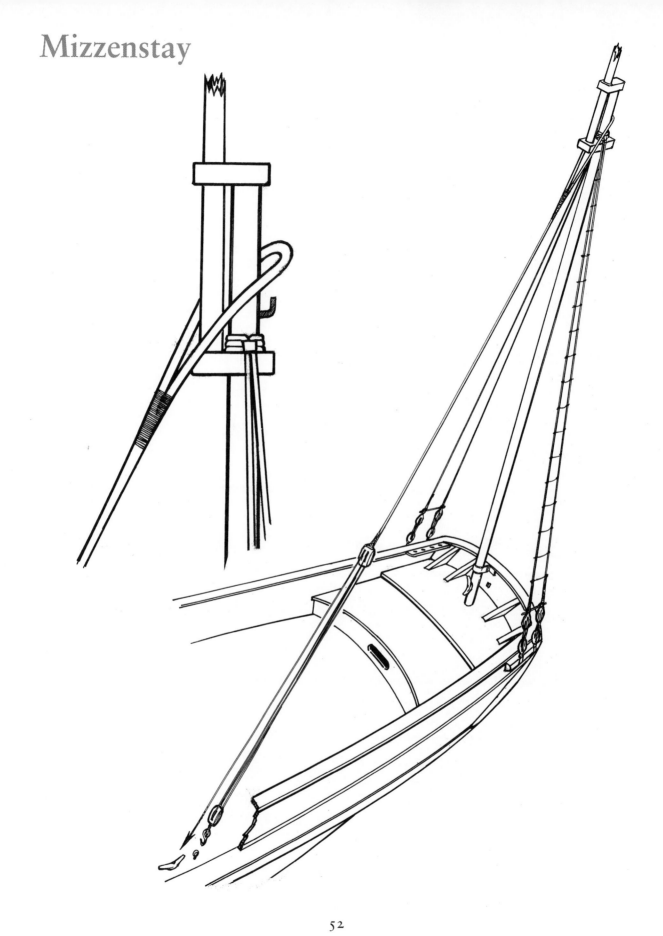

Bobstay & Bowsprit Shrouds

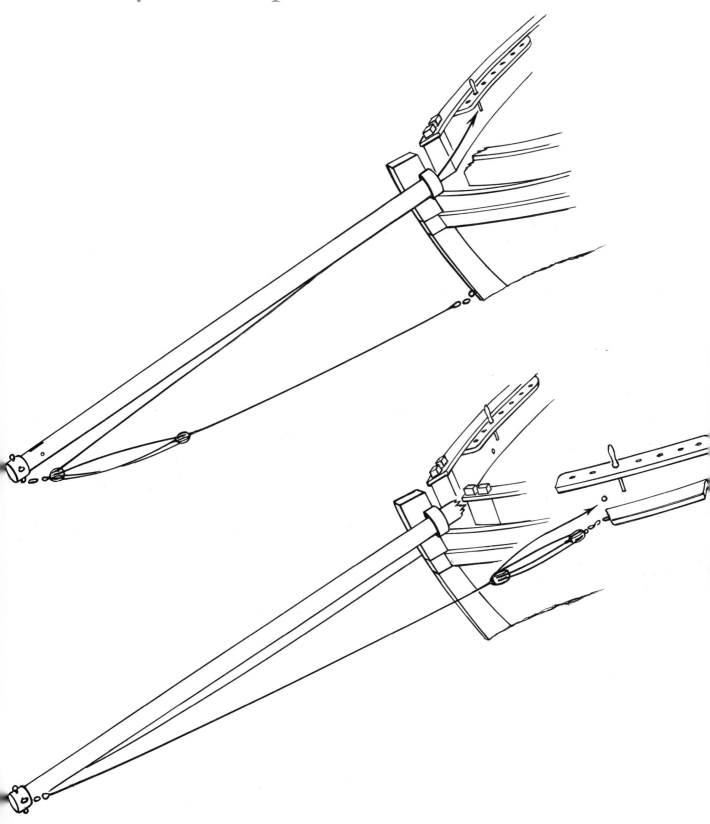

Jib

Halliard

Outhaul

Foresail Yard

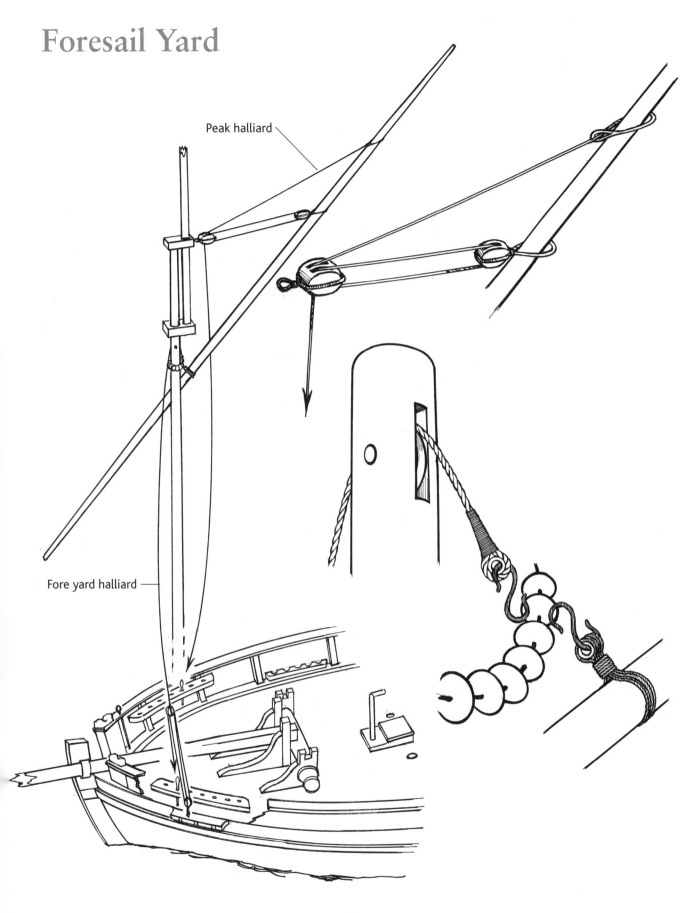

Peak halliard

Fore yard halliard

Foresail

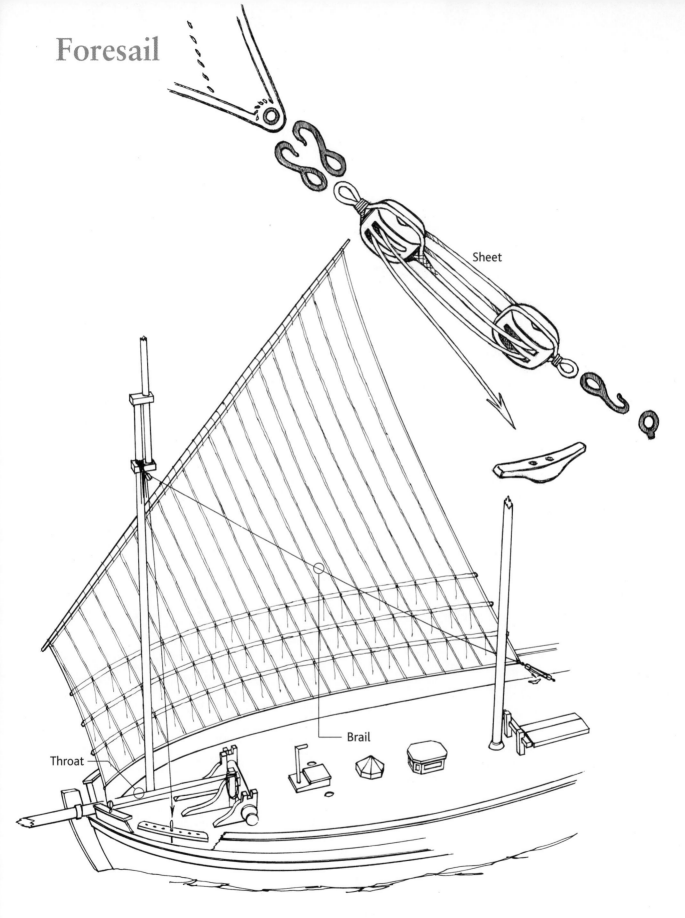

Sheet

Brail

Throat

Fore Topsail

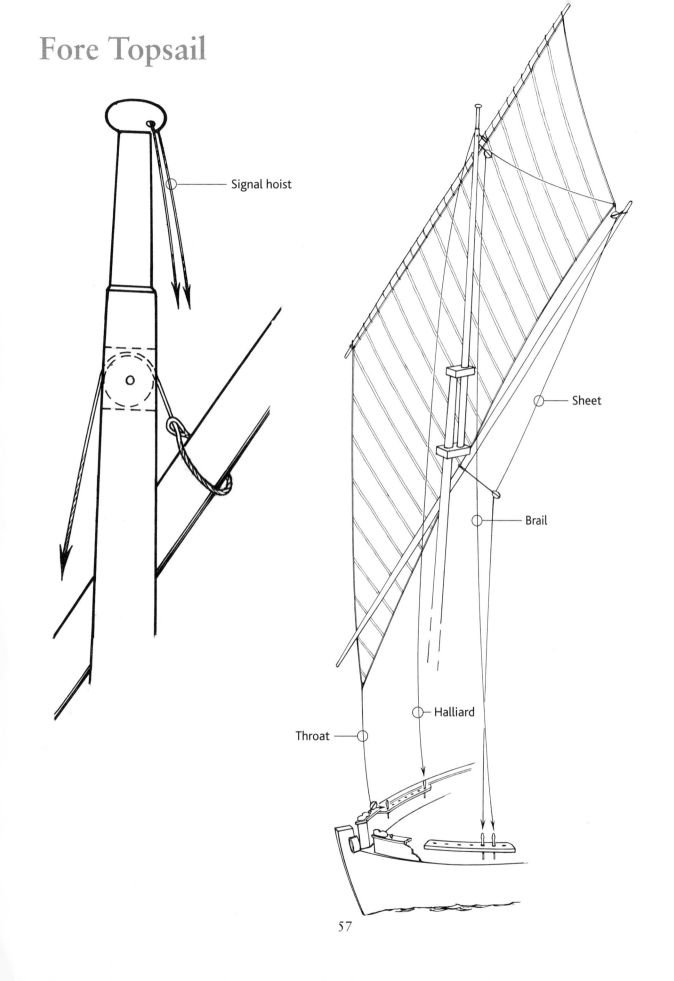

Signal hoist

Sheet

Brail

Halliard

Throat

Mainsail Yard

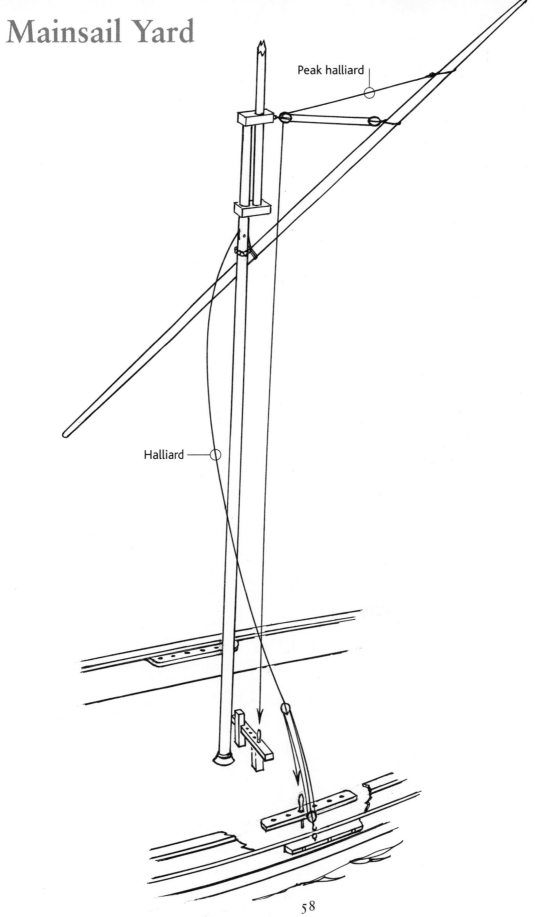

Peak halliard

Halliard

Mainsail

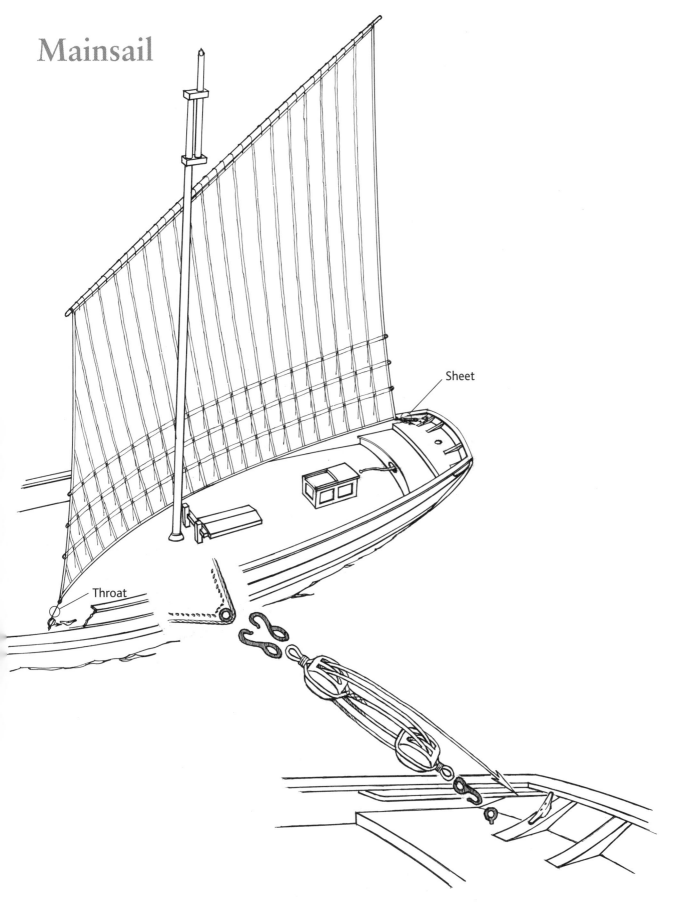

Sheet

Throat

Main Topsail

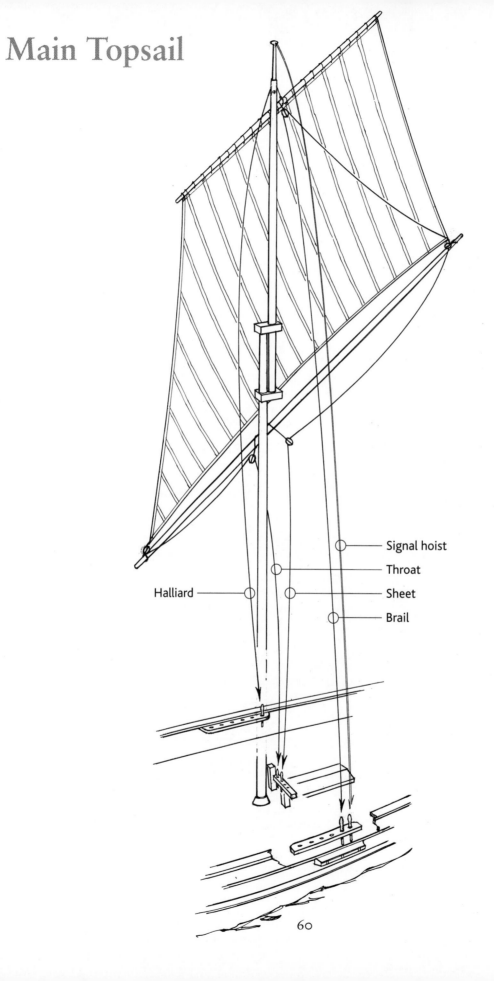

Signal hoist

Throat

Halliard

Sheet

Brail

Mizzen Yard & Sail

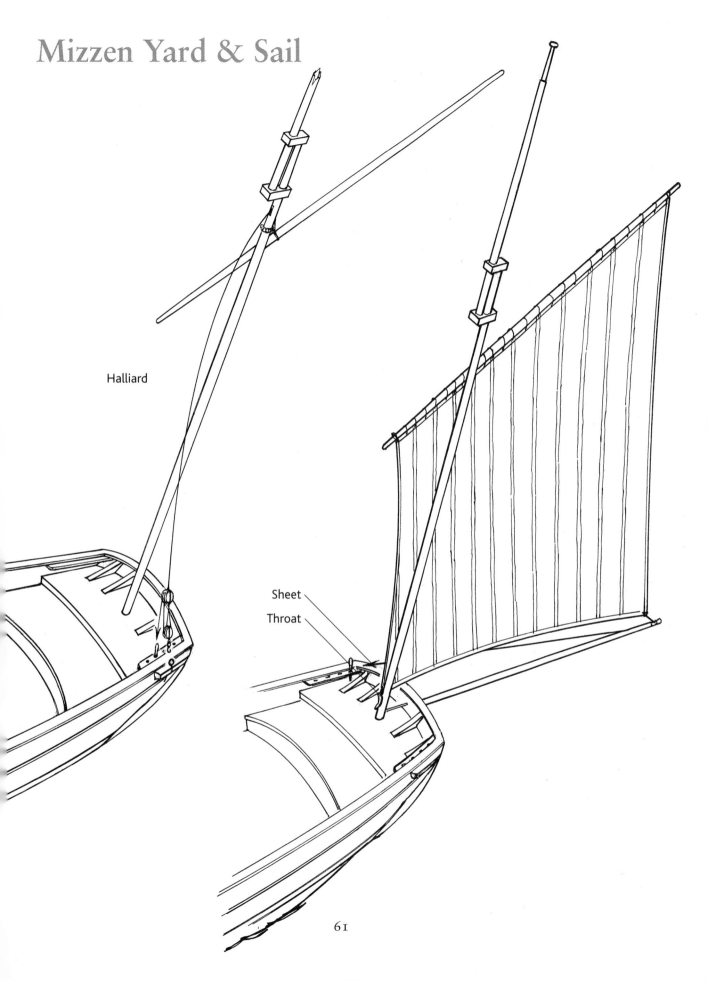

Halliard

Sheet

Throat

Bumpkin

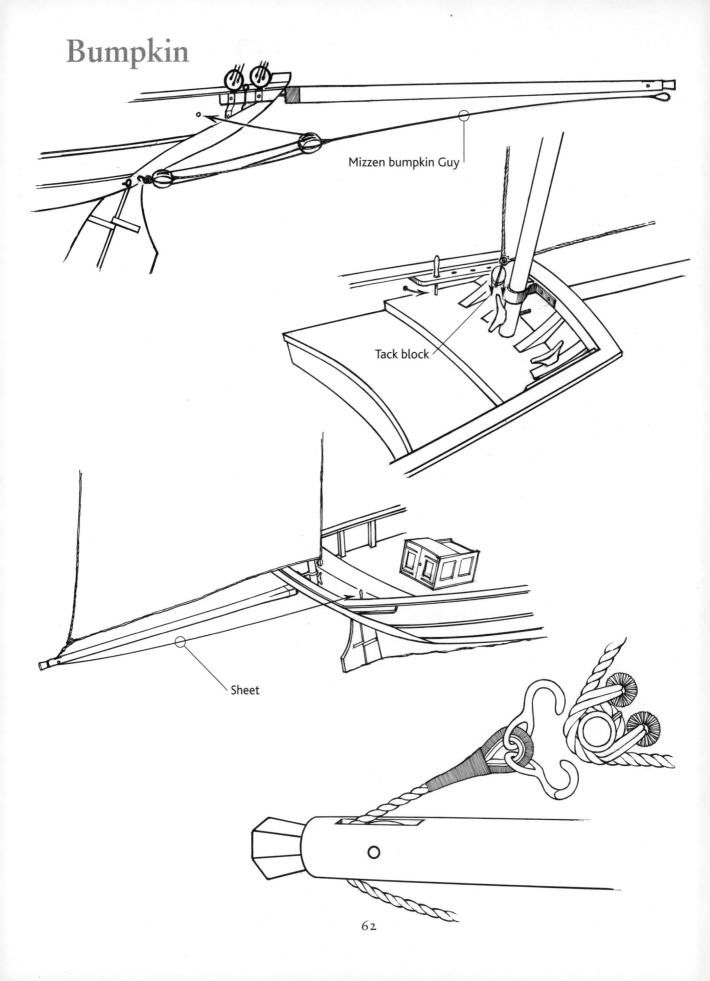

Mizzen bumpkin Guy

Tack block

Sheet

Mizzen Topsail

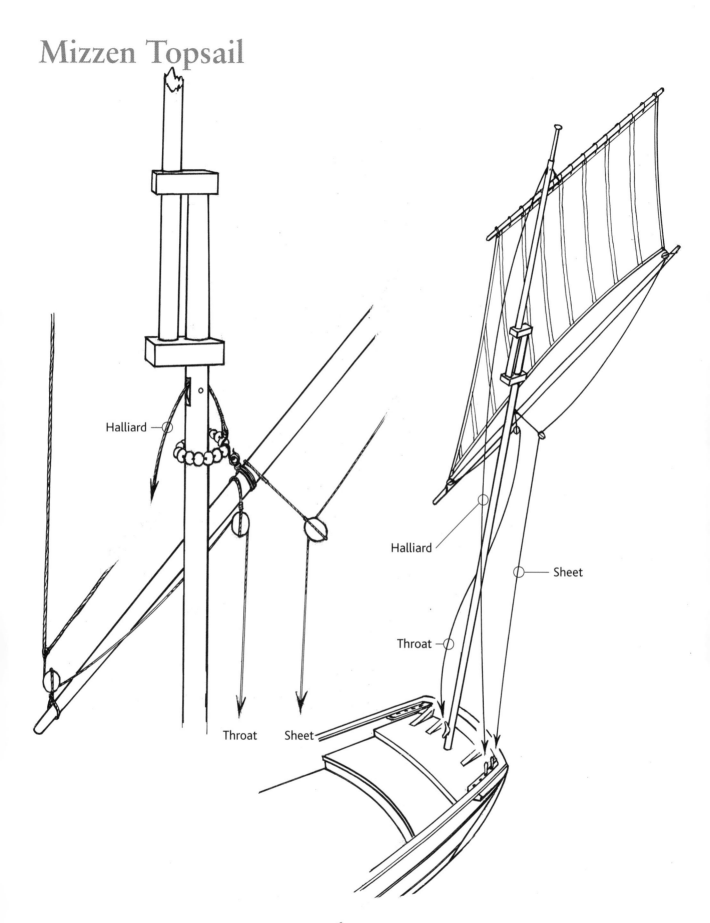

Halliard

Throat

Sheet

Halliard

Sheet

Throat

Anchor Gear

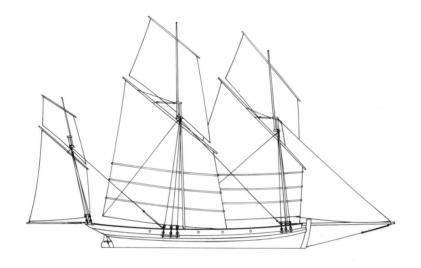

The
American
Schooner

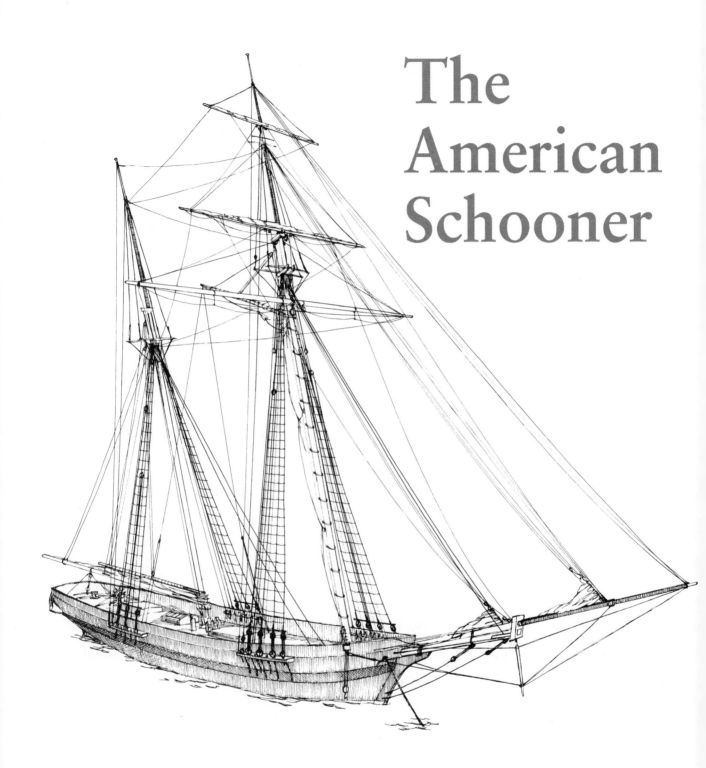

THE RIGGING PLAN for a typical American schooner is based on a model in the Naval Museum, Karlskrona, in Sweden. Although not an exact copy, she bears a close resemblance to the vessel that arrived in Karlskrona in the late summer of 1812 with vital supplies for the Swedish Navy. *Experiment*, as she was named, made a considerable impression on the Swedish Admiral Johan af Puke and later that year it was decided that she should be bought for the Navy. She became the prototype for four vessels built between 1831 and 1847 (namely *Falk*, *af Puke*, *L'Áigle* and *Activ*) and although the model was not entered in the Ships Models register until 1862, it probably dates from the time of the *Experiment*'s purchase.

Built in New York in 1808, the *Experiment* had an overall length of 73.3ft, a beam of 20.4ft, a displacement of 138 tons and carried six guns of varying calibre. One of the earliest of the ships later known as 'Baltimore clippers', she was one of the fastest vessels in the Swedish Navy and remained in the Navy in service until 1871. These fore-and-aft schooners were fast to windward and they became the perfect model of the privateer. But with their low freeboard, relatively light build and tall rig they were vulnerable in a sea and certainly difficult to handle; nor had they the displacement to carry much armament. But the raked masts, carrying a cloud of canvas, and the long, lean hulls made for very fast if dangerous ships, and the unsettled political situation during the French Revolution and the Napoleonic Wars led to an enormous demand for fast vessels suitable for blockade running, reconnaissance, smuggling and privateering; these American schooners, renowned for their speed and excellent sailing qualities, were the perfect answer and were in great demand by the European navies. Not all were purchased, however, and a number were inevitably taken as prizes.

The *Prince de Neufchatel*, one of the largest specialist-built American privateers, so impressed the Royal Navy that a copy was planned, but the end of the War of 1812 put such plans on hold. Even after the end of the war, however, these vessels played a significant role in the development of the sailing ship and throughout the nineteenth century their lines and rig exerted influence on both the ships of the Royal Navy and on merchant vessel design, and in the field of competitive yachting they became the forerunners of the elegant boats that would race for the America's Cup.

Profile & Deck Plan

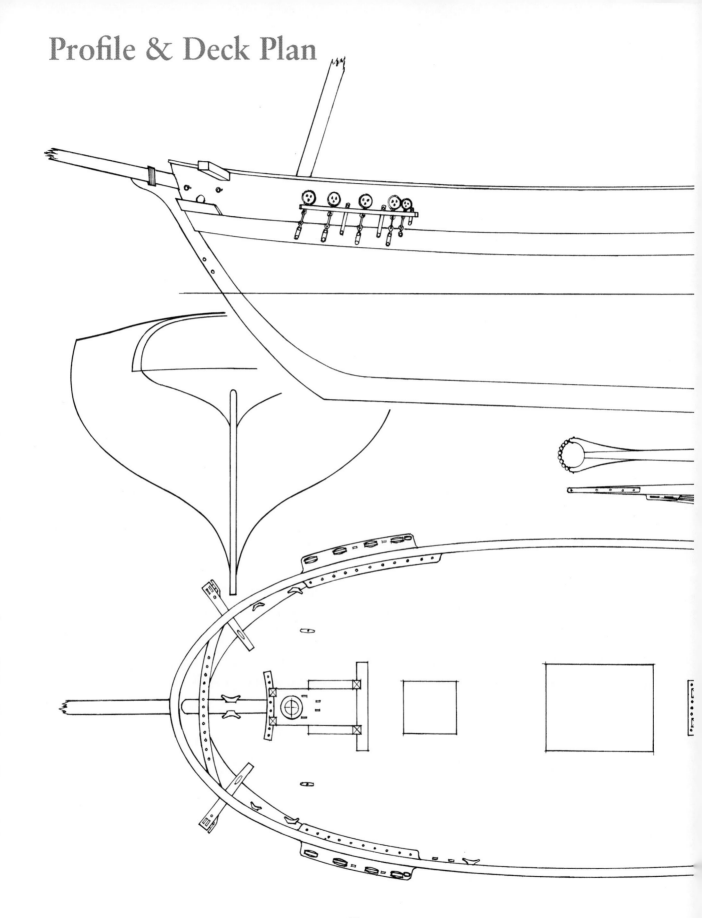

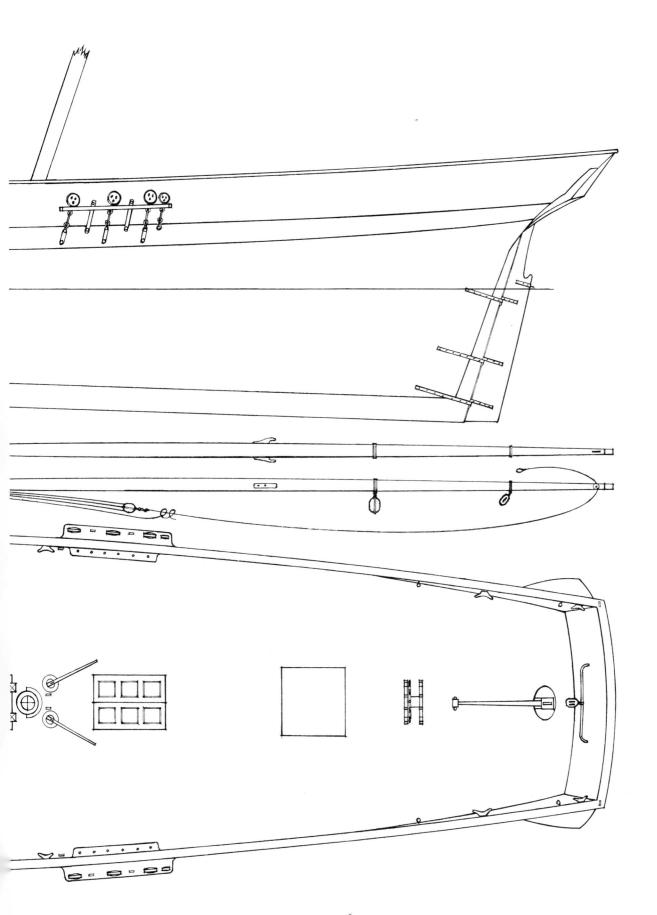

Belaying Plan

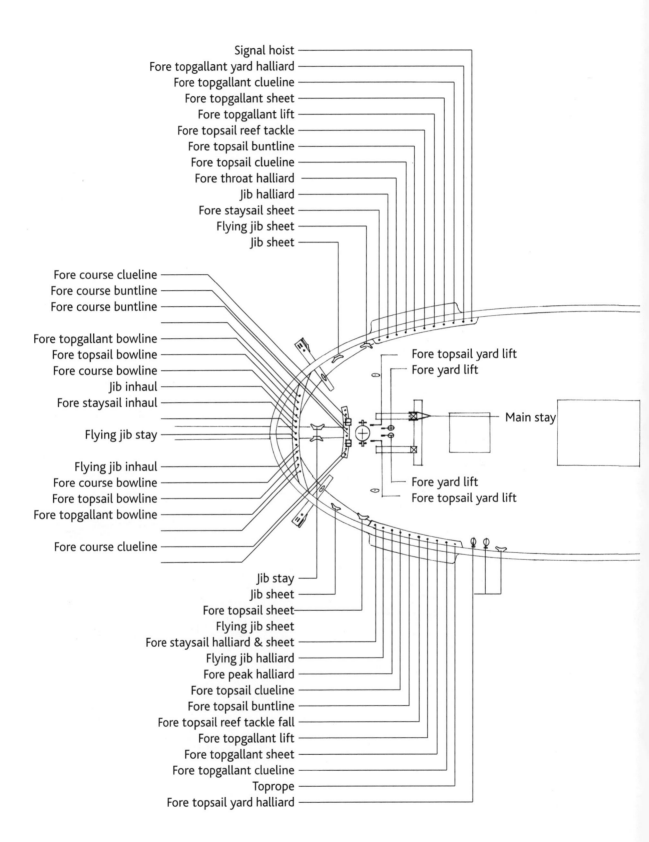

Signal hoist
Fore topgallant yard halliard
Fore topgallant clueline
Fore topgallant sheet
Fore topgallant lift
Fore topsail reef tackle
Fore topsail buntline
Fore topsail clueline
Fore throat halliard
Jib halliard
Fore staysail sheet
Flying jib sheet
Jib sheet

Fore course clueline
Fore course buntline
Fore course buntline

Fore topgallant bowline
Fore topsail bowline
Fore course bowline
Jib inhaul
Fore staysail inhaul

Flying jib stay

Flying jib inhaul
Fore course bowline
Fore topsail bowline
Fore topgallant bowline

Fore course clueline

Fore topsail yard lift
Fore yard lift

Main stay

Fore yard lift
Fore topsail yard lift

Jib stay
Jib sheet
Fore topsail sheet
Flying jib sheet
Fore staysail halliard & sheet
Flying jib halliard
Fore peak halliard
Fore topsail clueline
Fore topsail buntline
Fore topsail reef tackle fall
Fore topgallant lift
Fore topgallant sheet
Fore topgallant clueline
Toprope
Fore topsail yard halliard

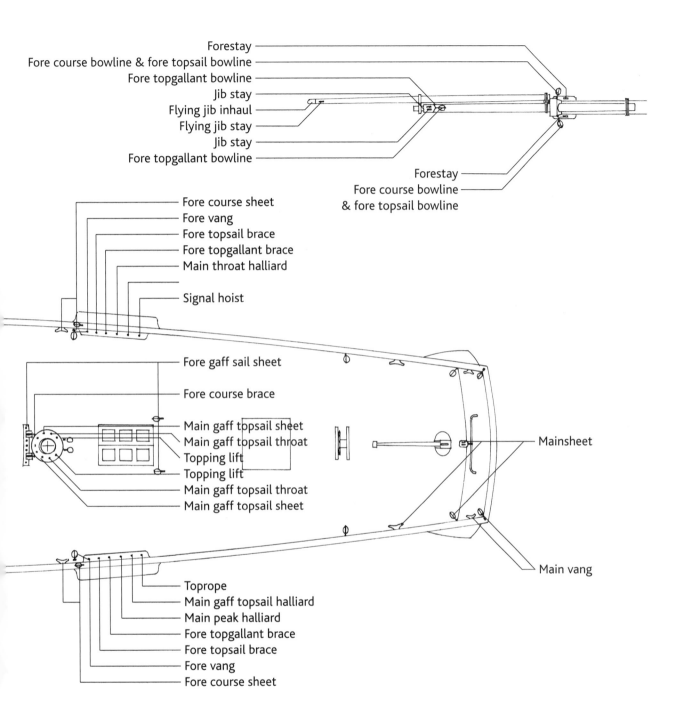

Forestay

Fore course bowline & fore topsail bowline

Fore topgallant bowline

Jib stay

Flying jib inhaul

Flying jib stay

Jib stay

Fore topgallant bowline

Forestay

Fore course bowline
& fore topsail bowline

Fore course sheet

Fore vang

Fore topsail brace

Fore topgallant brace

Main throat halliard

Signal hoist

Fore gaff sail sheet

Fore course brace

Main gaff topsail sheet

Main gaff topsail throat

Topping lift

Topping lift

Main gaff topsail throat

Main gaff topsail sheet

Mainsheet

Main vang

Toprope

Main gaff topsail halliard

Main peak halliard

Fore topgallant brace

Fore topsail brace

Fore vang

Fore course sheet

Fore Channels

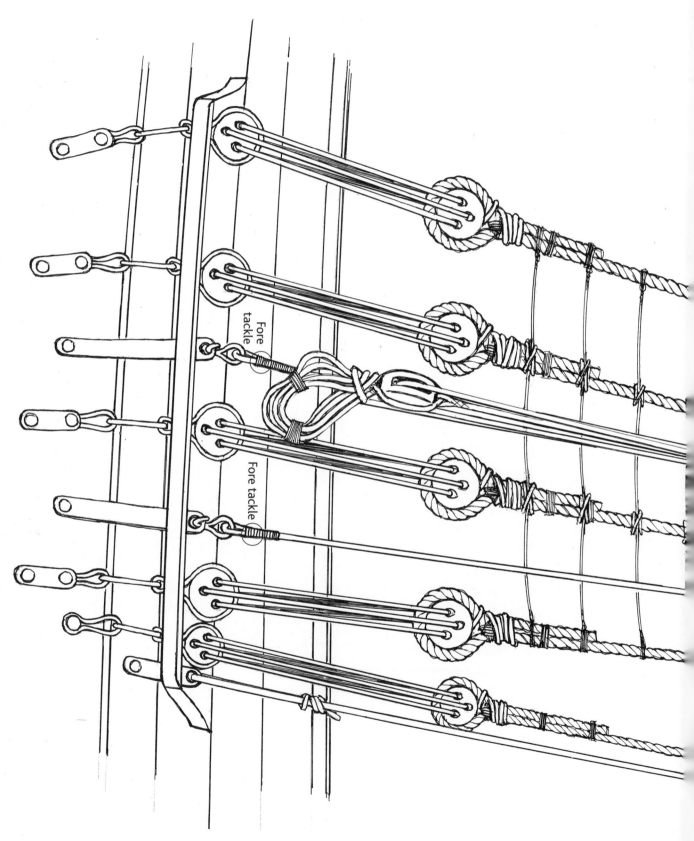

Fore tackle

Fore tackle

Main Channels

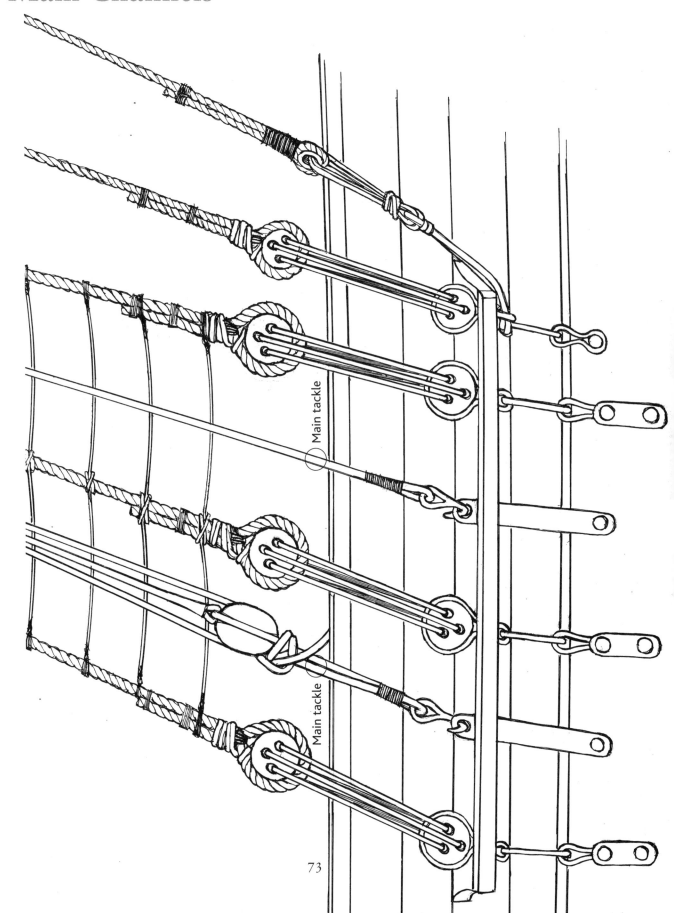

Main tackle

Main tackle

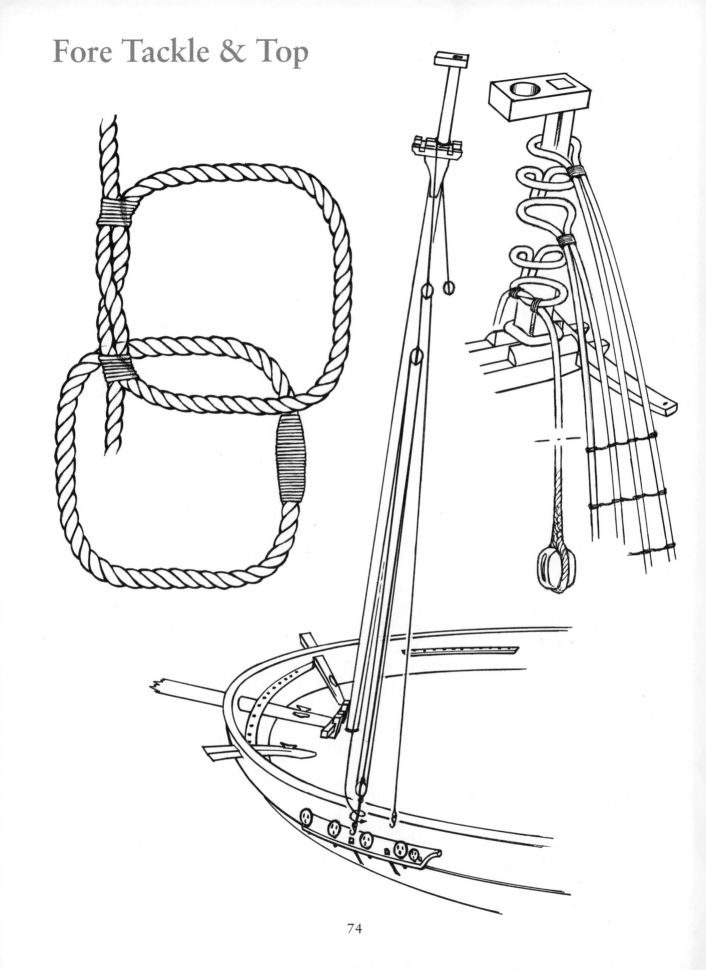

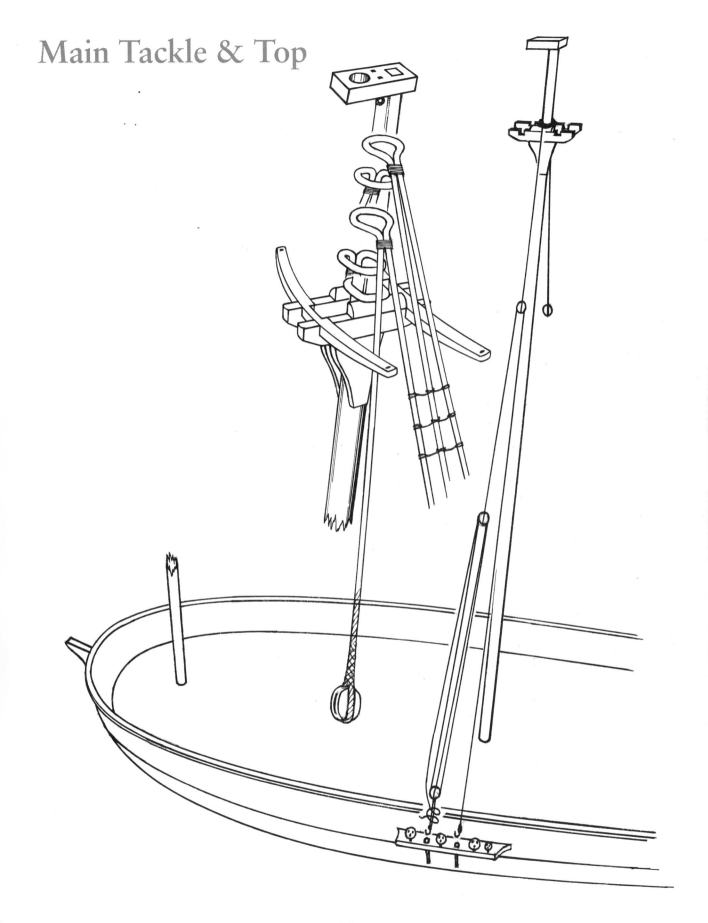

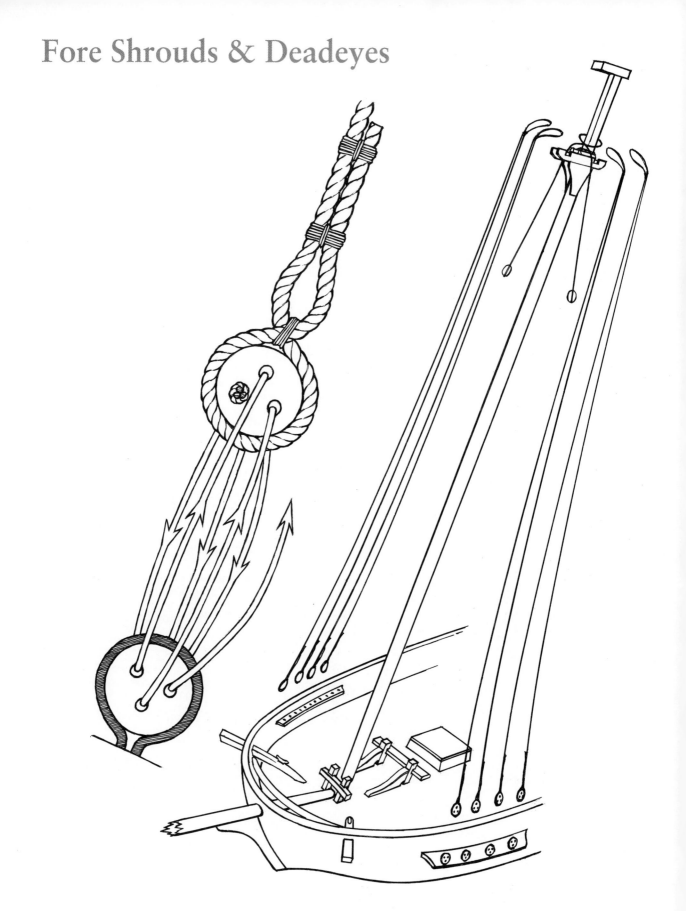

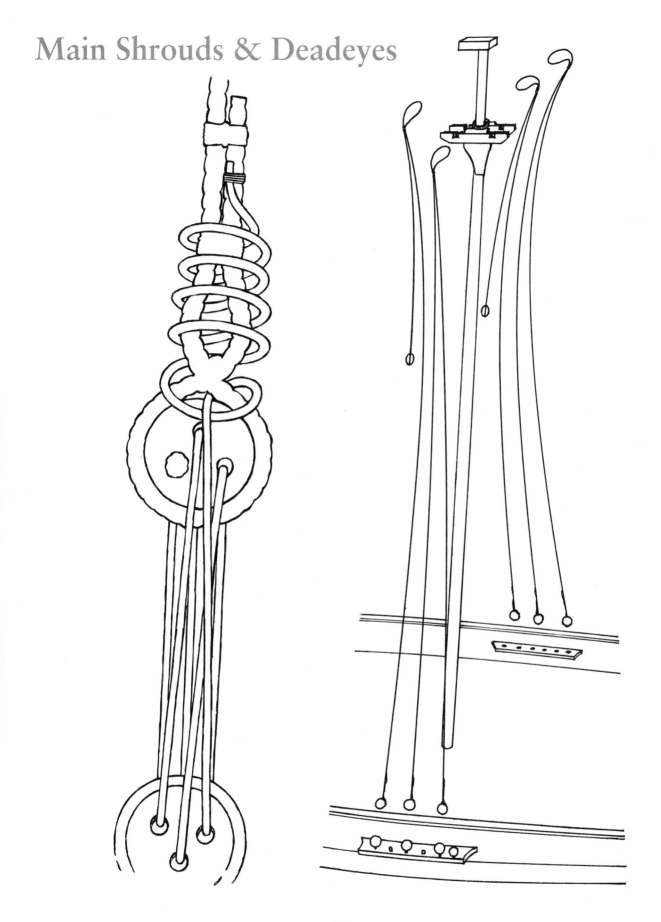

Toprope

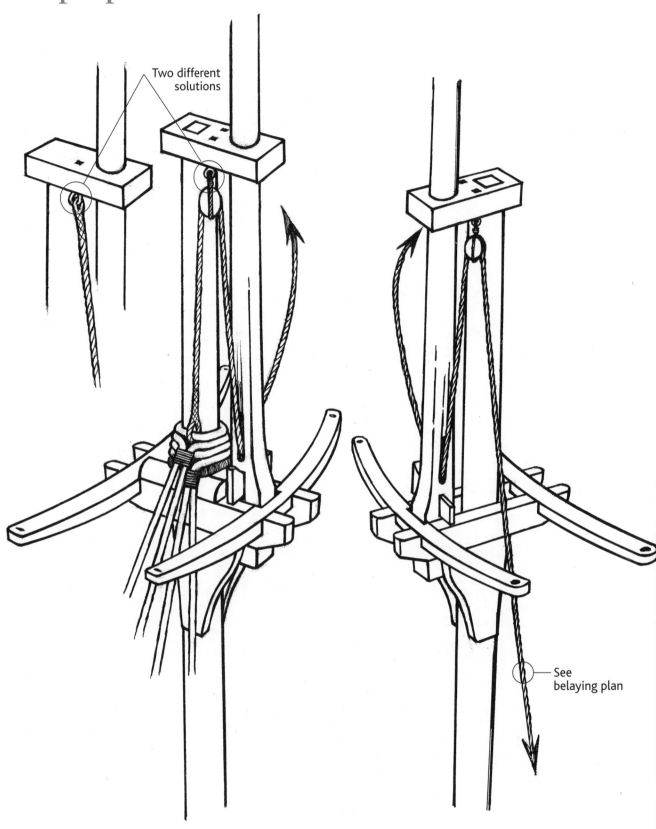

Two different solutions

See belaying plan

78

Forestay

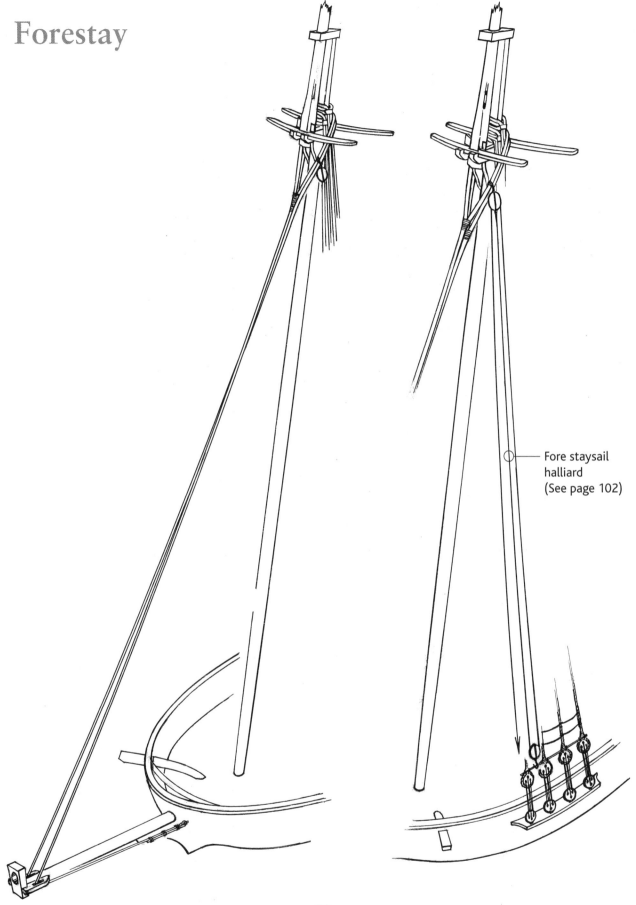

Fore staysail
halliard
(See page 102)

Mainstay

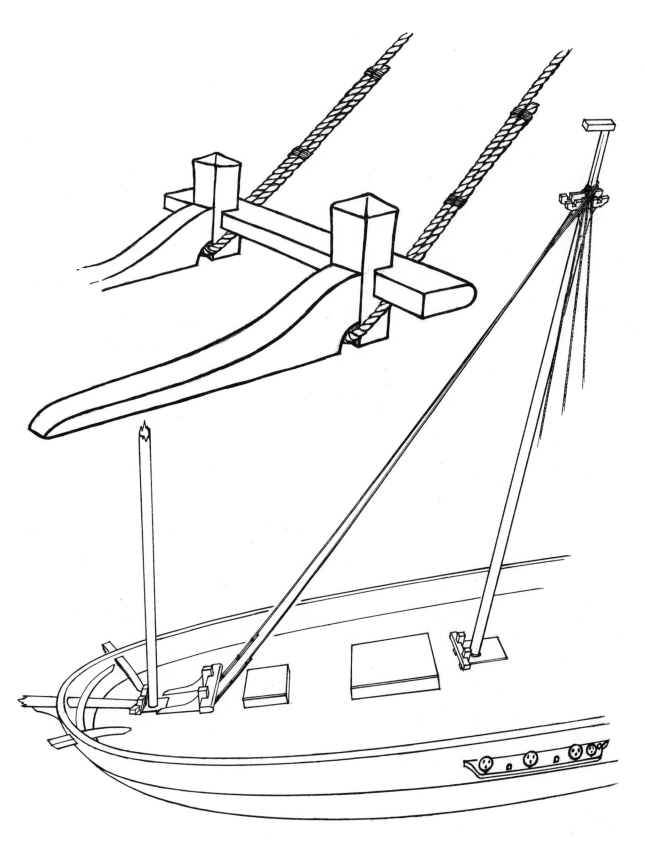

Fore Topmast &
Topgallant Shrouds

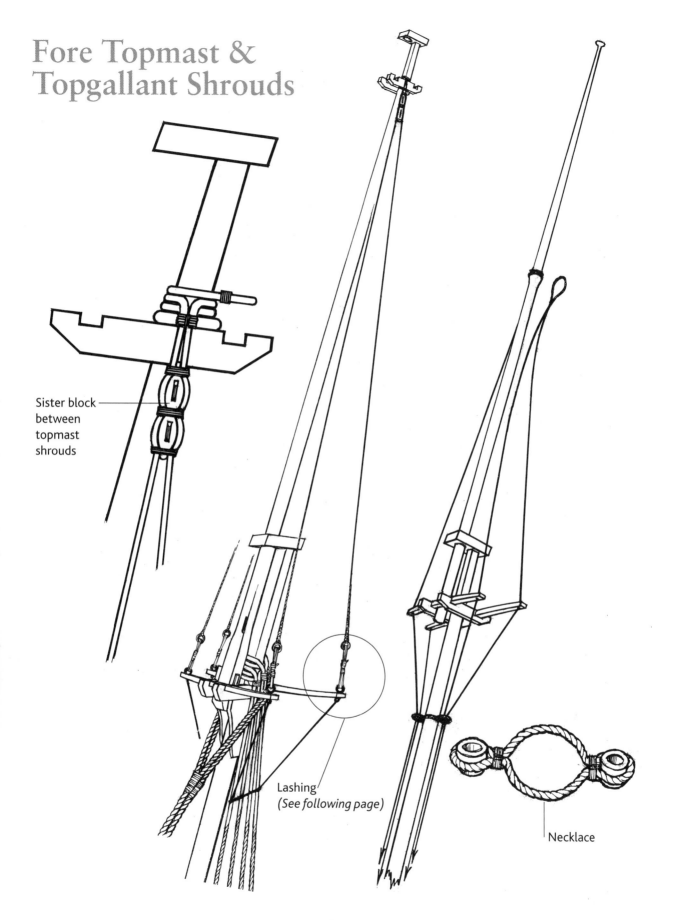

Sister block
between
topmast
shrouds

Lashing
(See following page)

Necklace

Main Topmast Shrouds

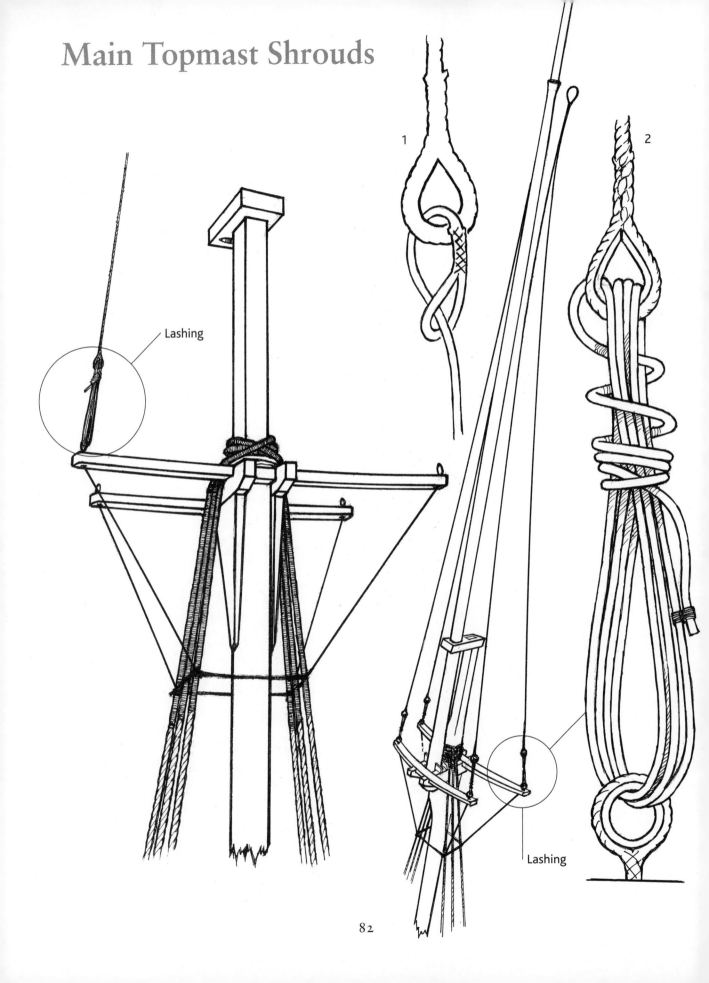

Lashing

1

2

Lashing

Backstays

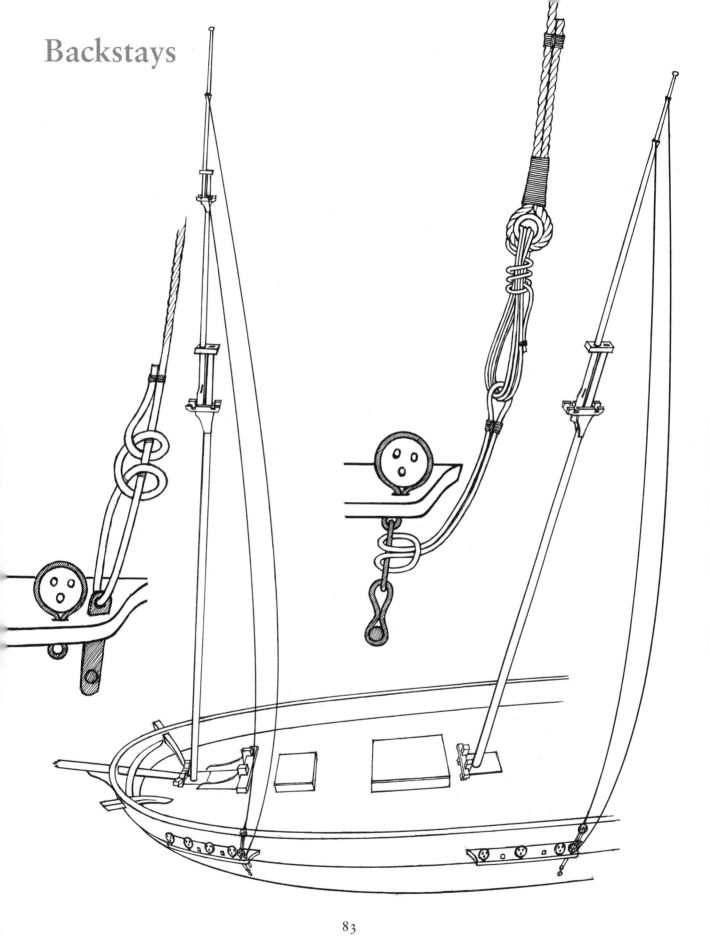

Bobstay

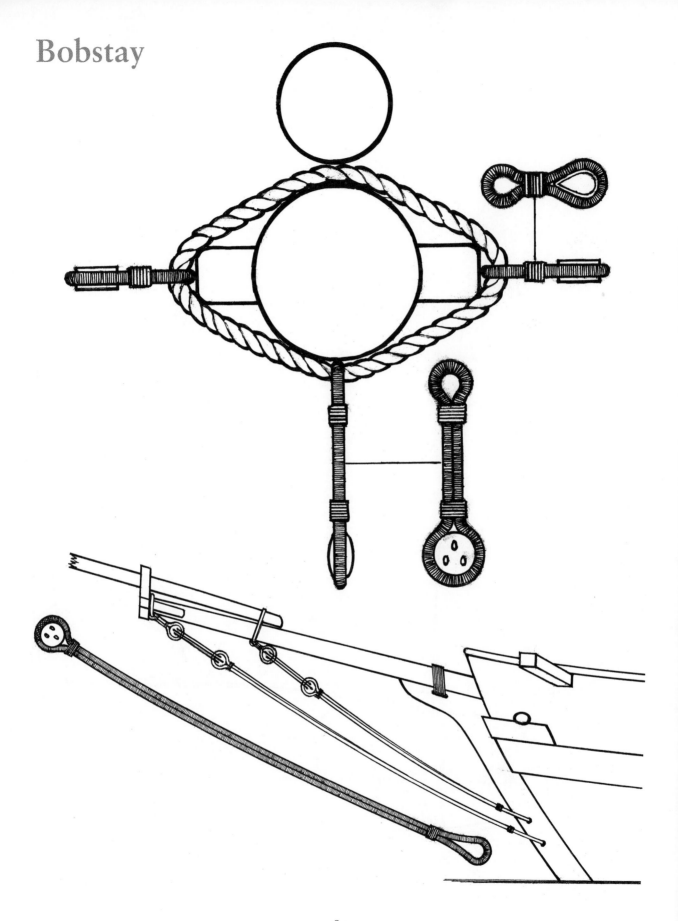

Bowsprit Guy,
Martingale Stays,
Jibboom Guys

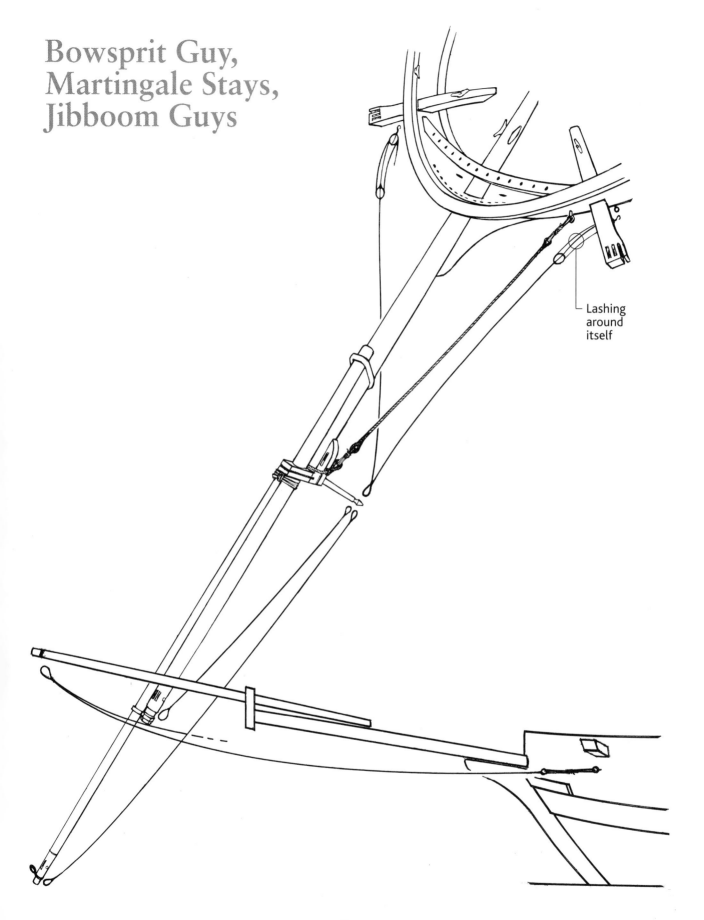

Lashing
around
itself

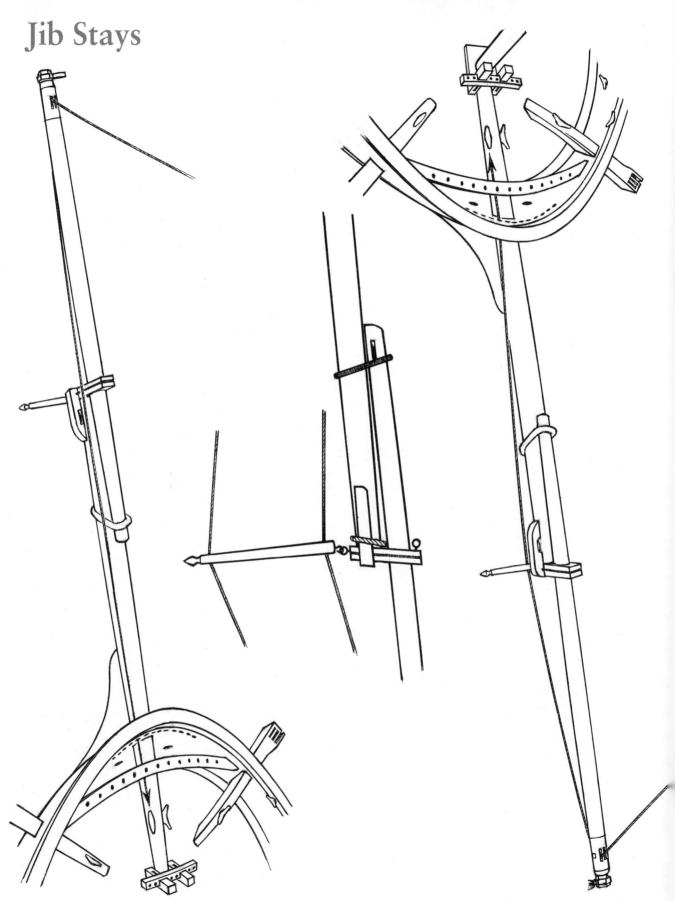

Flying Jib Stay

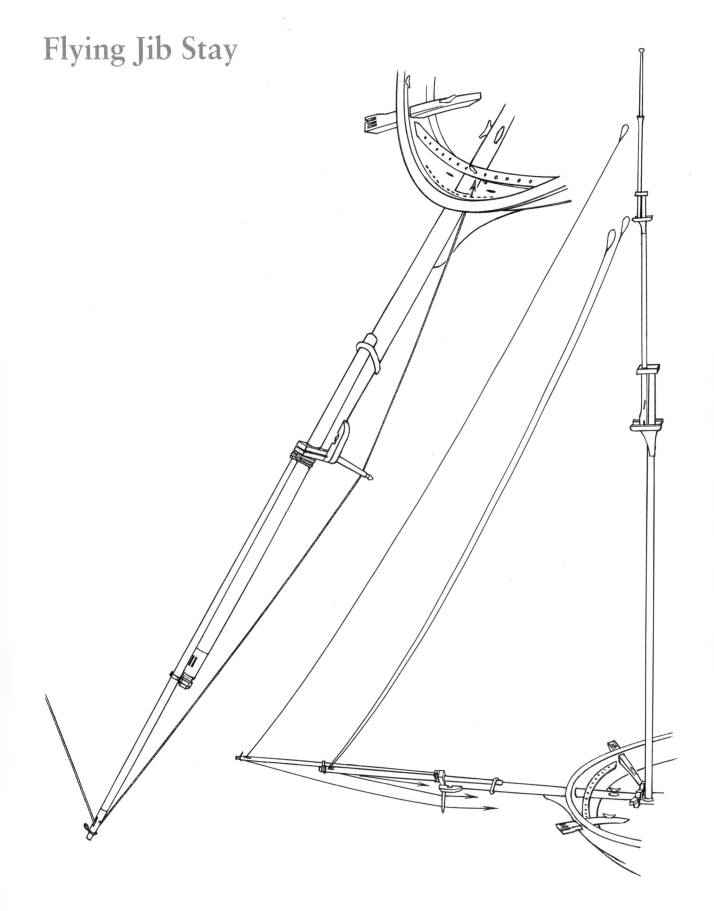

Main Topmast & Topgallant Stay

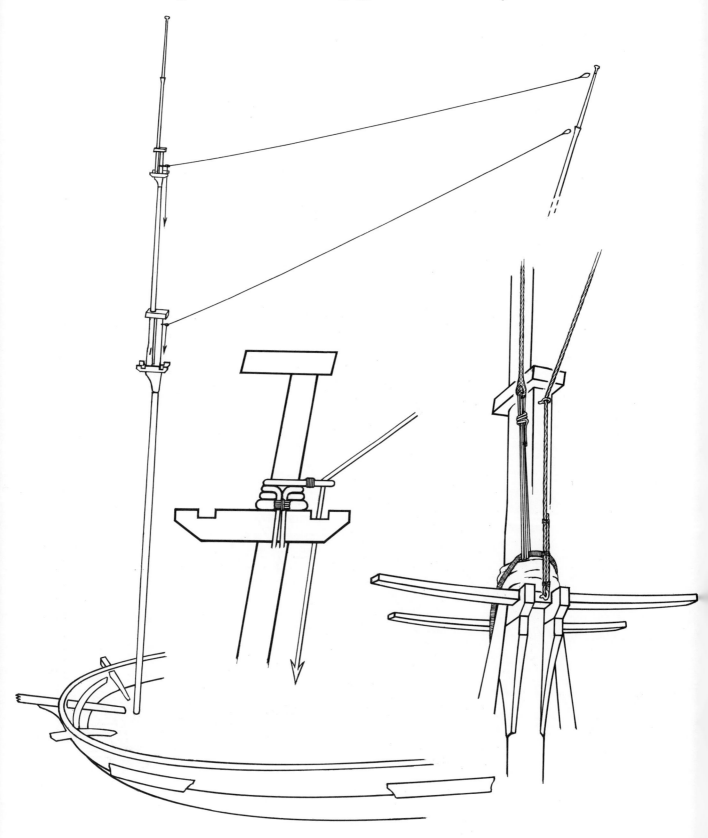

Foremast Yards

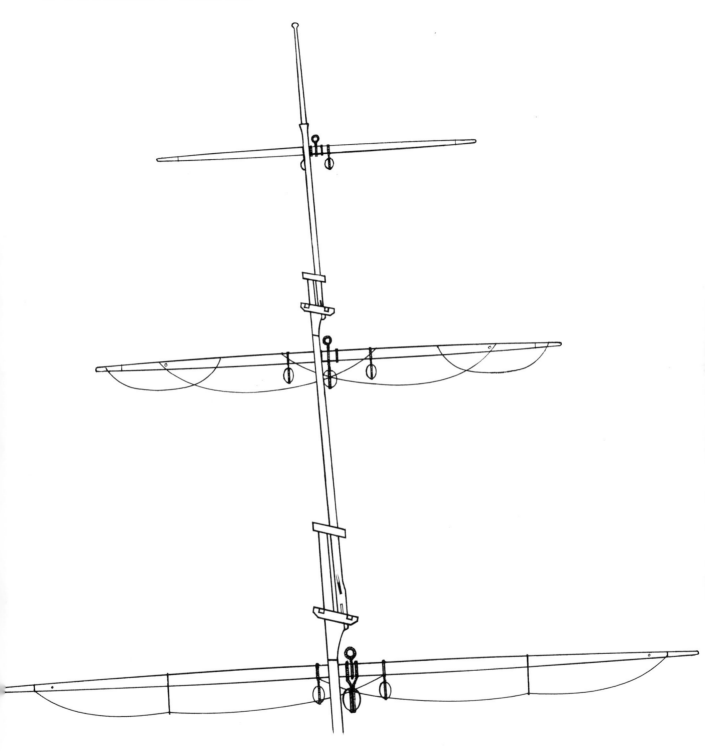

Fore yard Sling, Topsail & Topgallant Yard Halliards

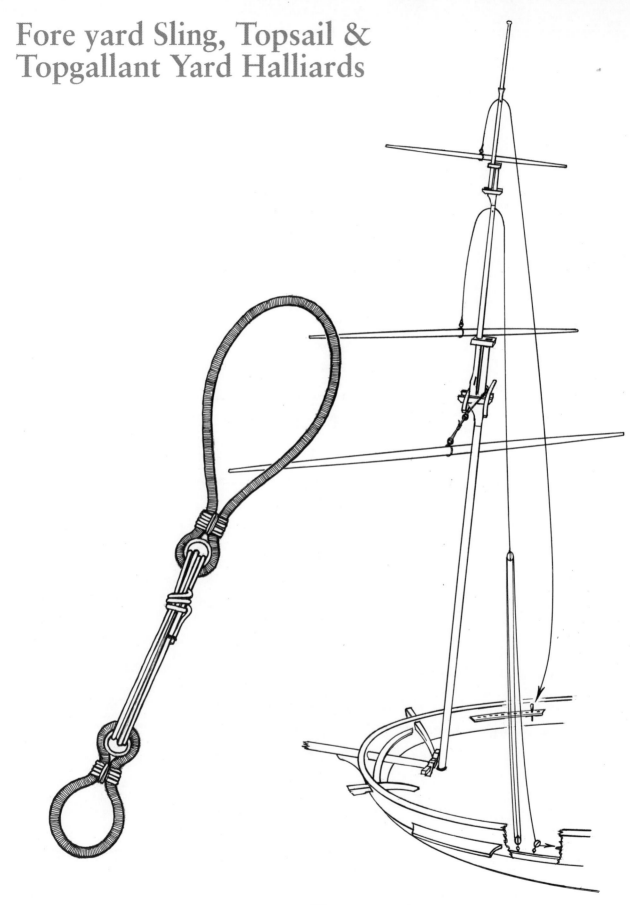

Lifts

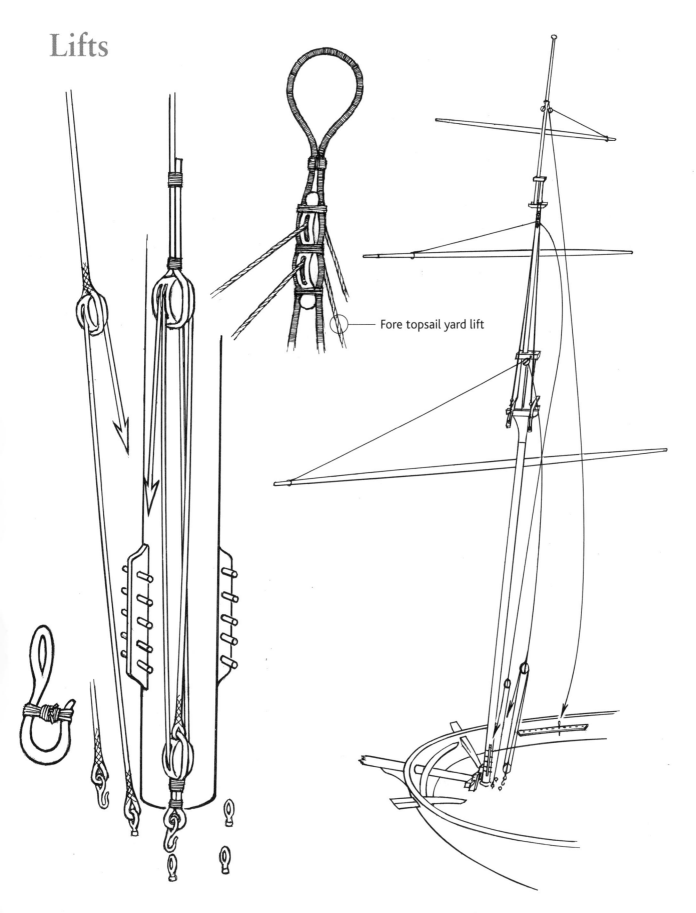

Fore topsail yard lift

Braces

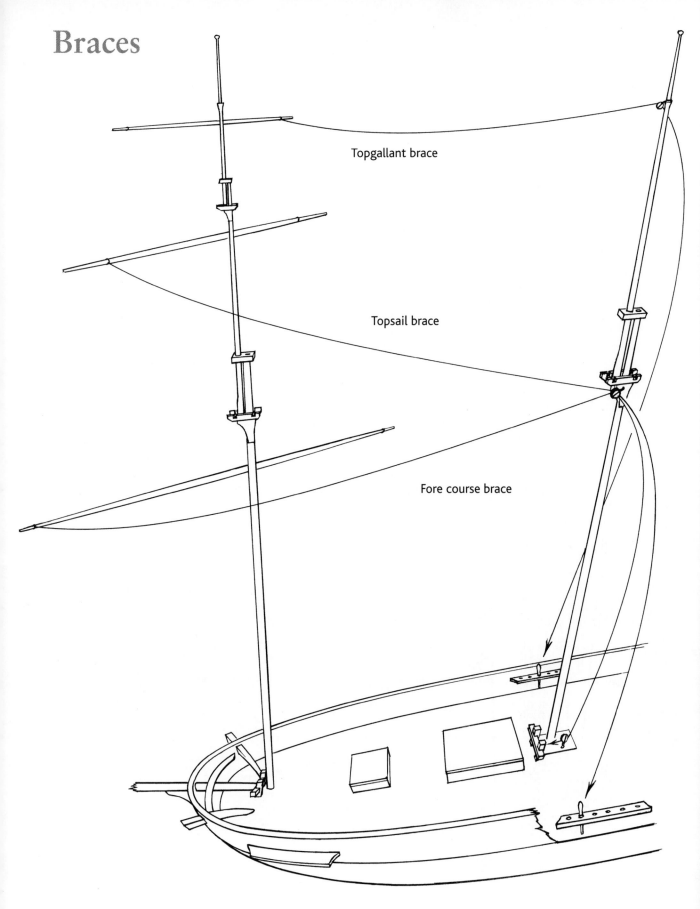

Topgallant brace

Topsail brace

Fore course brace

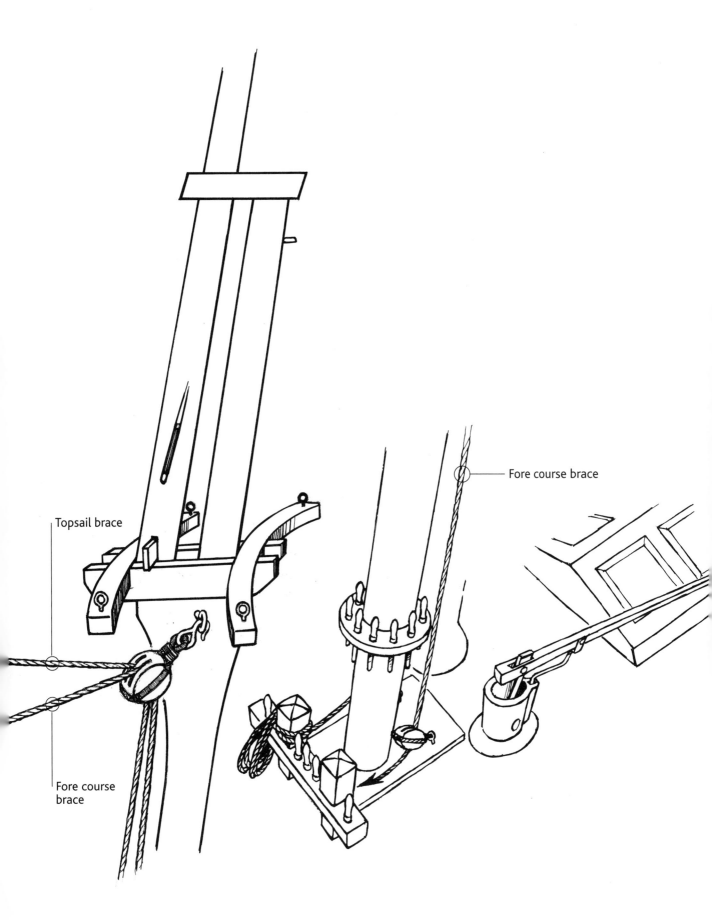

Topsail brace

Fore course brace

Fore course brace

Fore Throat & Peak Halliards

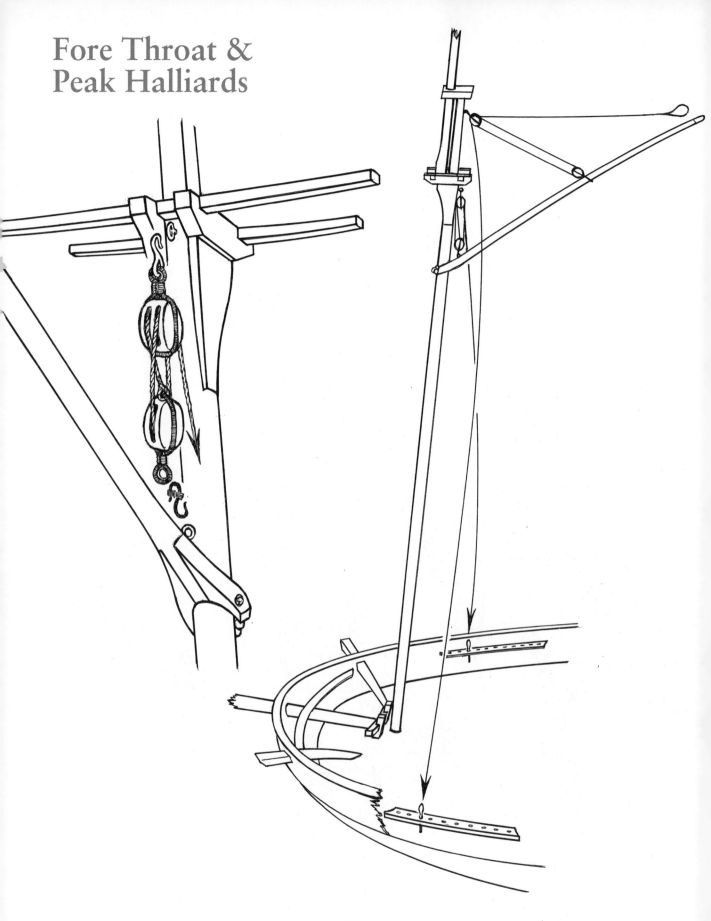

Fore Vangs

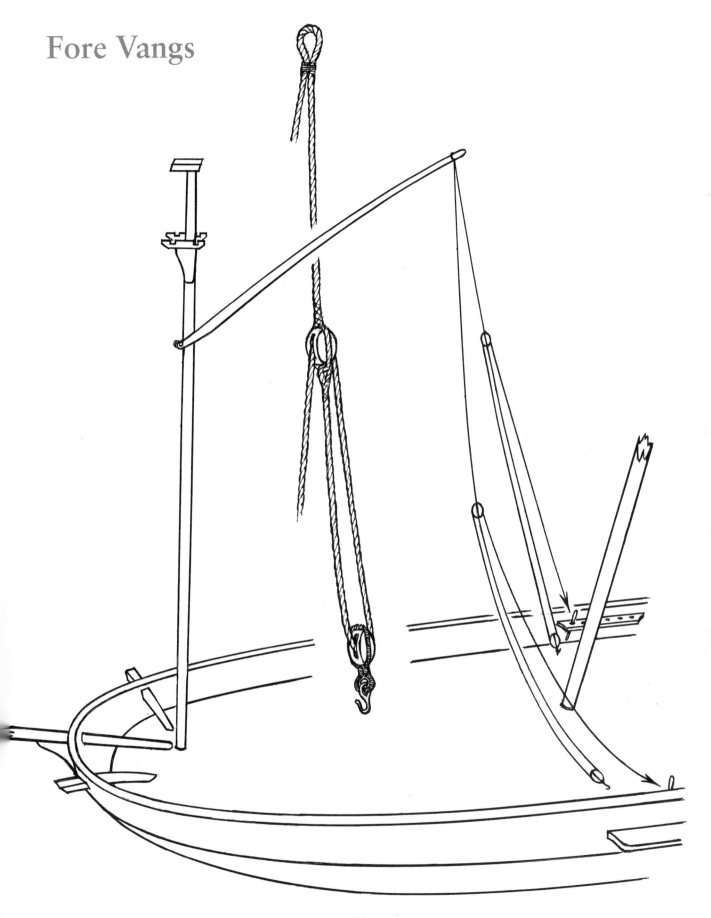

Main Throat & Peak Halliards, Main Vangs

Main Boom Topping Lift

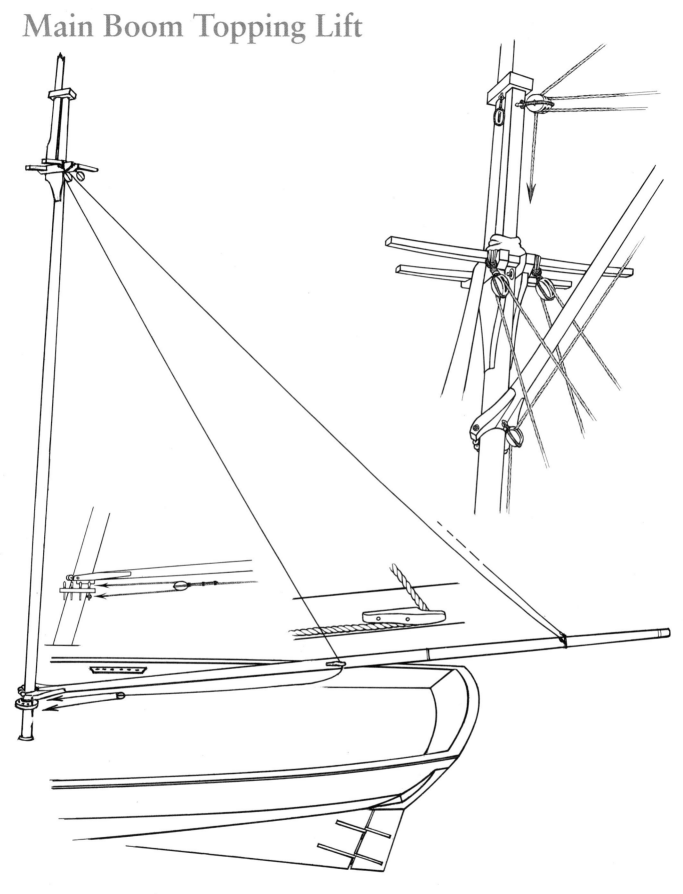

Mainsheet & Steering Gear

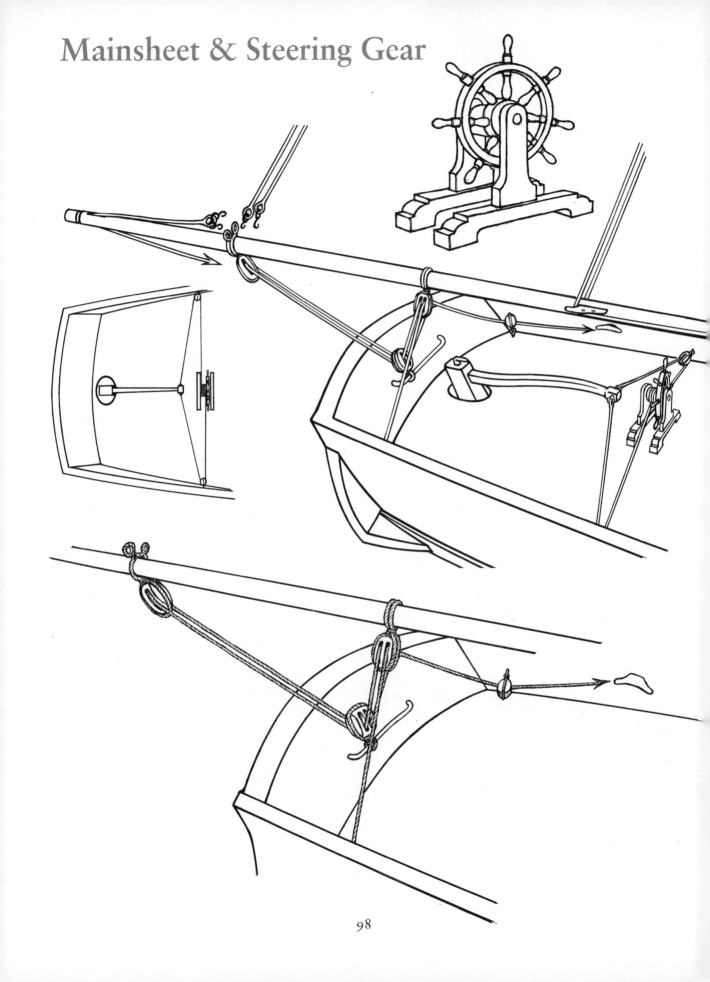

Mainsail Outhaul

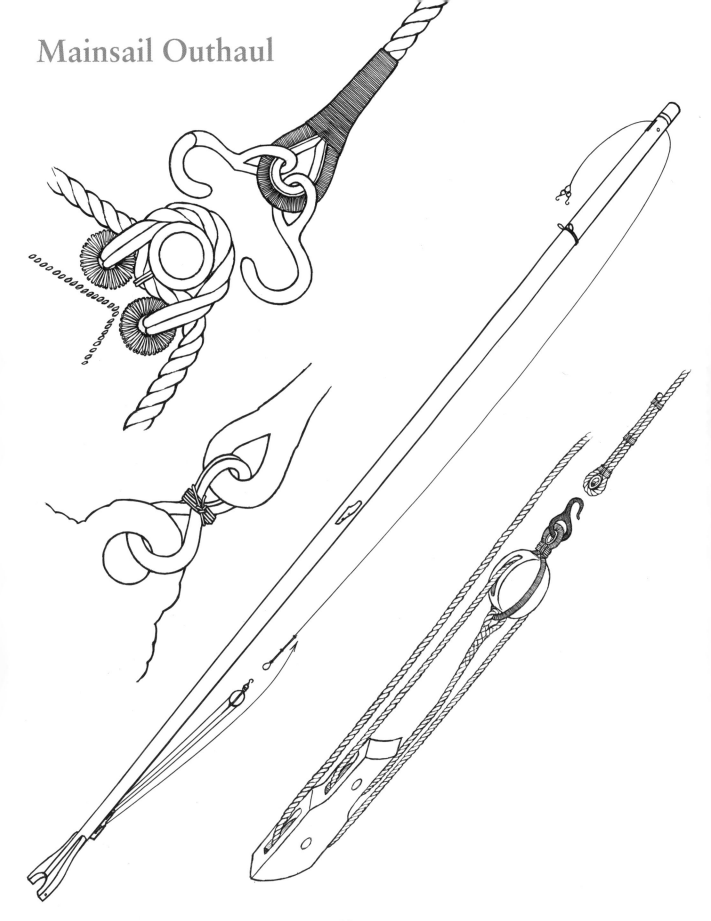

Flying Jib

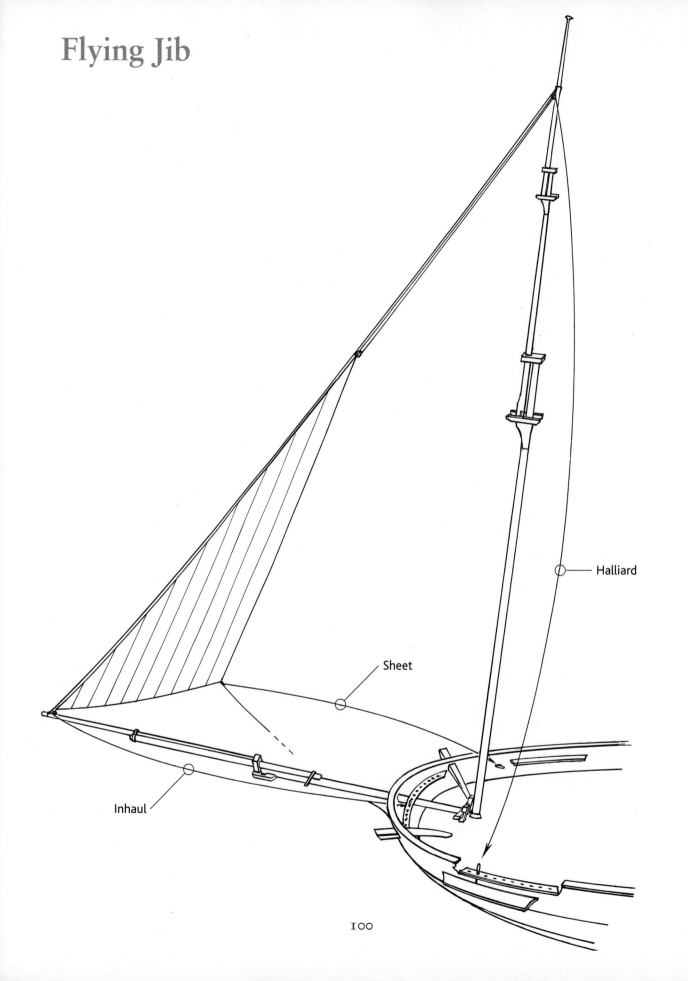

Halliard

Sheet

Inhaul

Jib

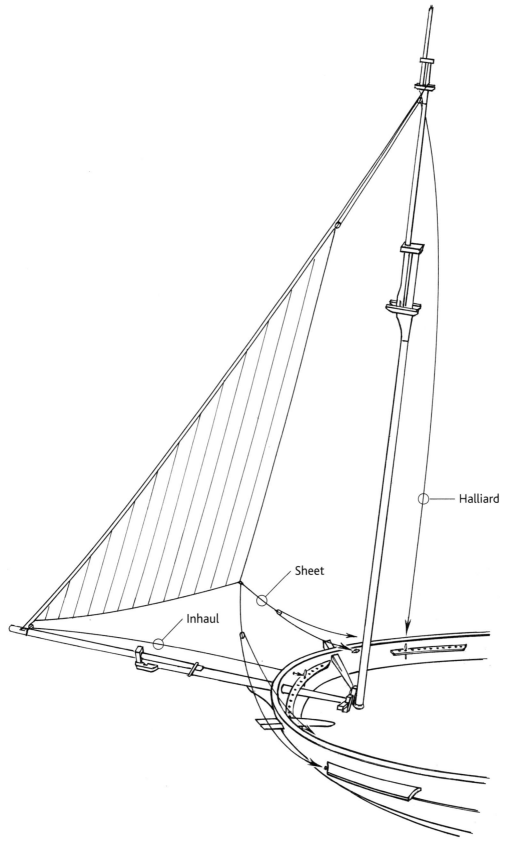

Halliard

Sheet

Inhaul

Fore Staysail

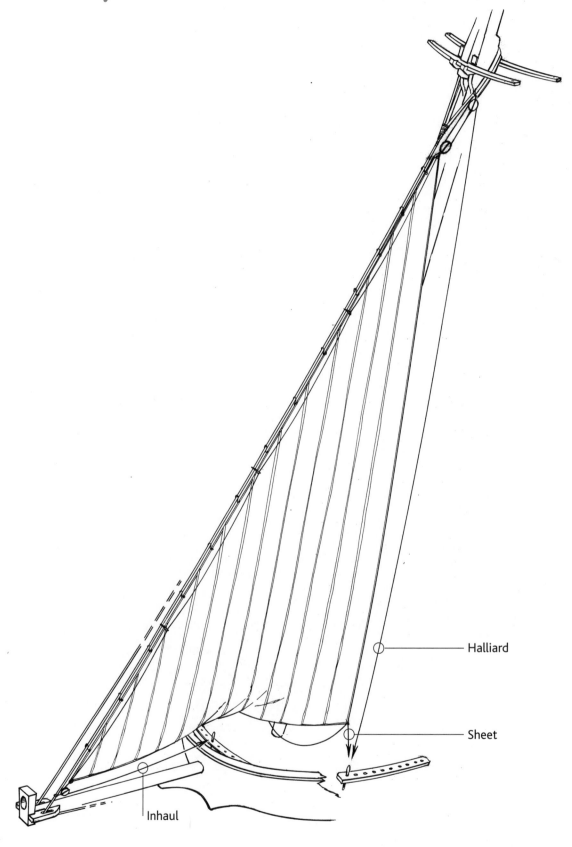

Halliard

Sheet

Inhaul

Fore Course Clueline, Buntline & Sheet

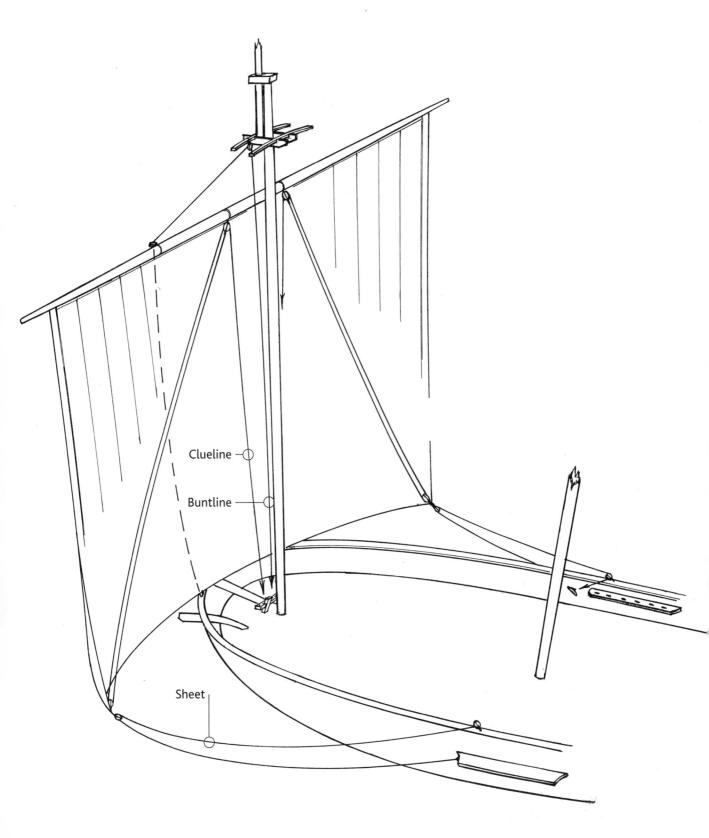

Clueline

Buntline

Sheet

Fore Course Bowlines

Fore Topsail Clueline
& Reef Tackle

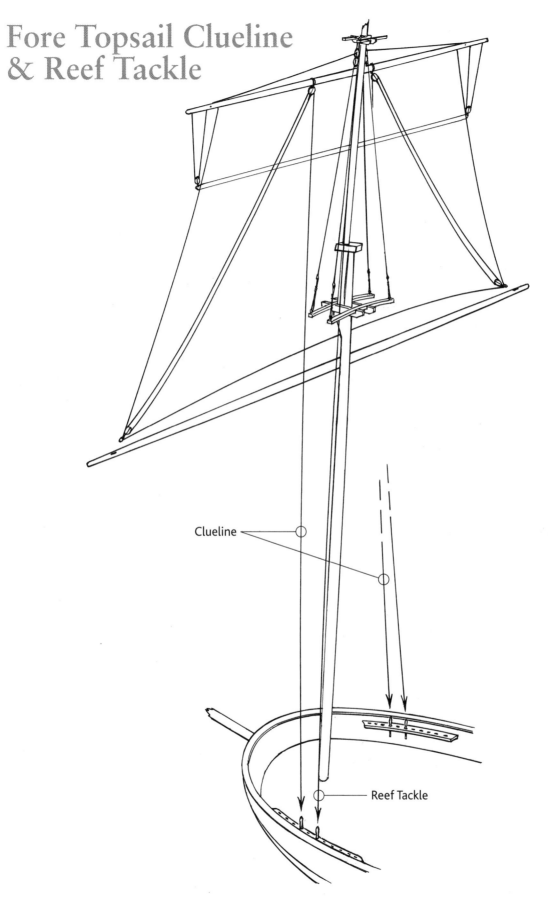

Clueline

Reef Tackle

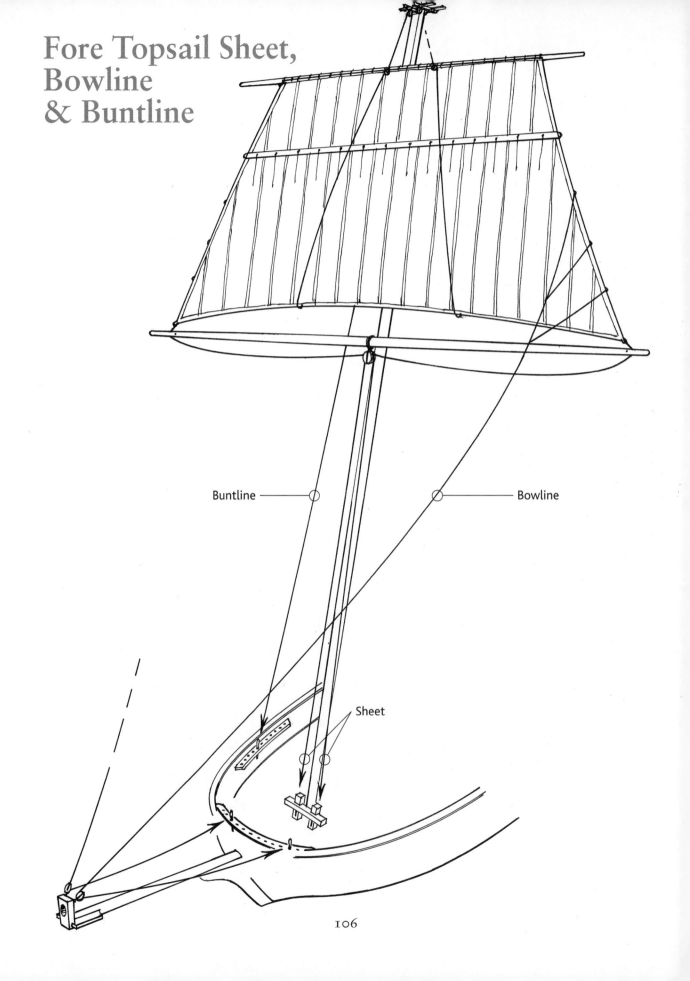

Fore Topsail Sheet, Bowline & Buntline

Buntline

Bowline

Sheet

Fore Topgallant Clueline,
Bowline & Sheet

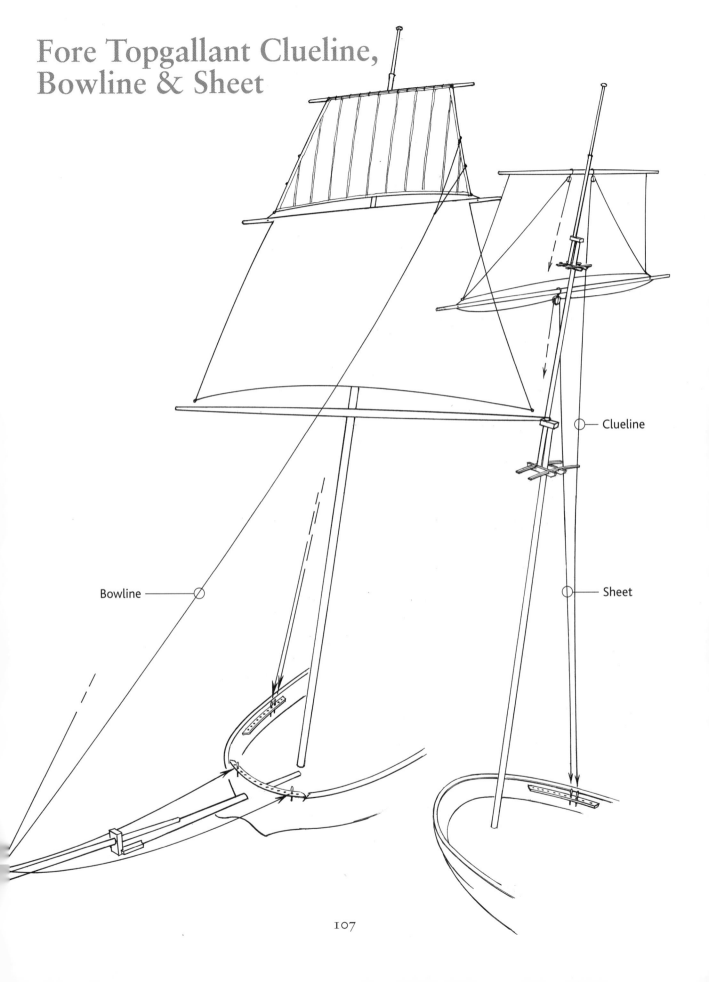

Clueline

Bowline

Sheet

Fore Gaff Sail

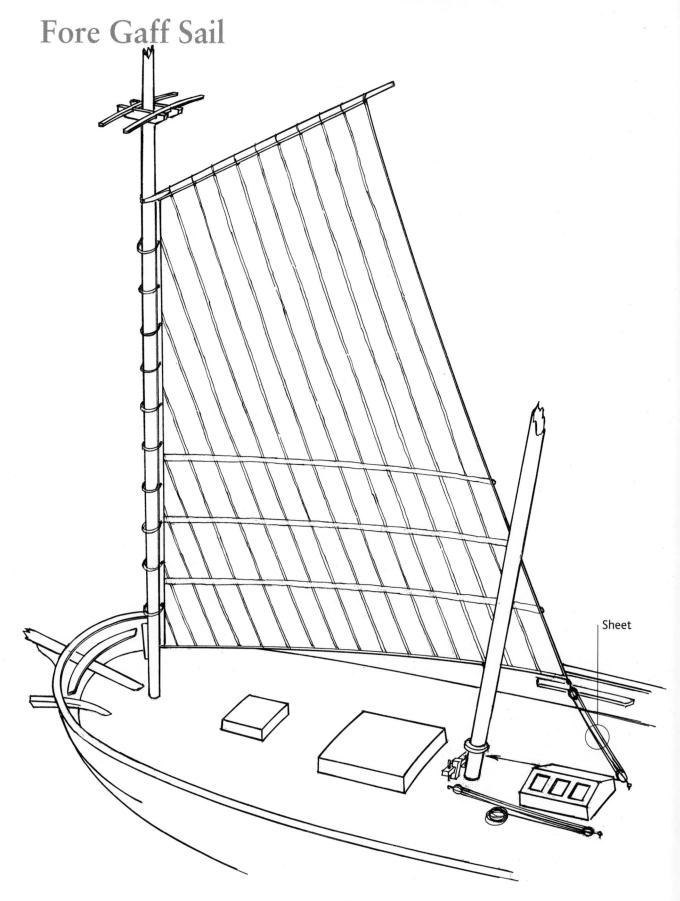

Sheet

Main Gaff Topsail, Swedish Fashion

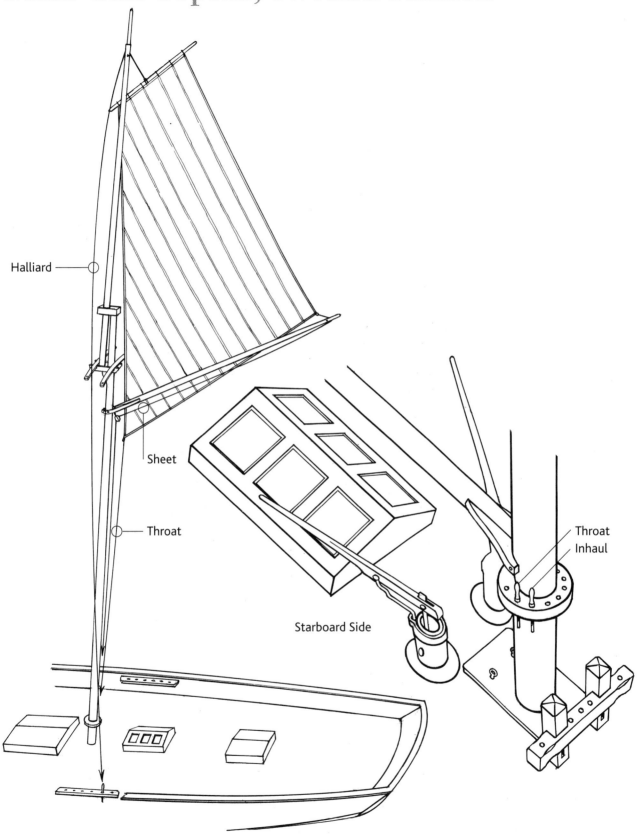

Halliard

Sheet

Throat

Starboard Side

Throat
Inhaul

Main Gaff Topsail, American Fashion

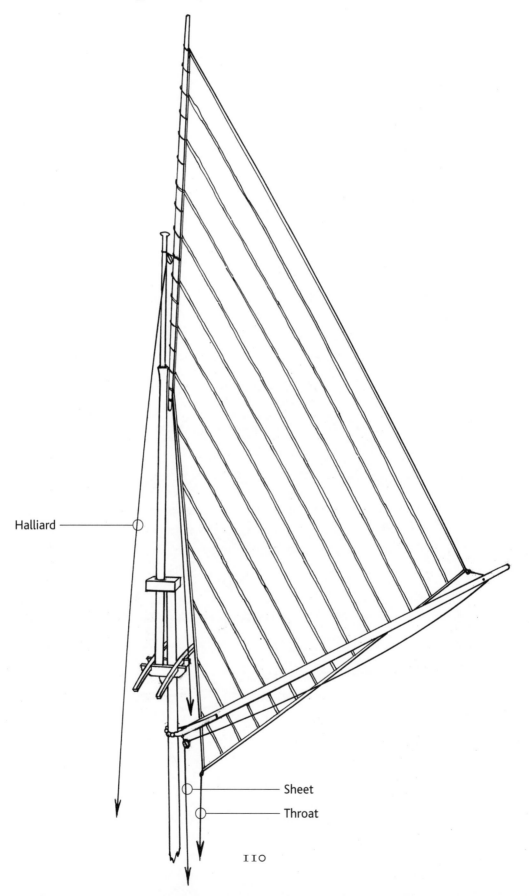

Halliard

Sheet

Throat

Mainsail

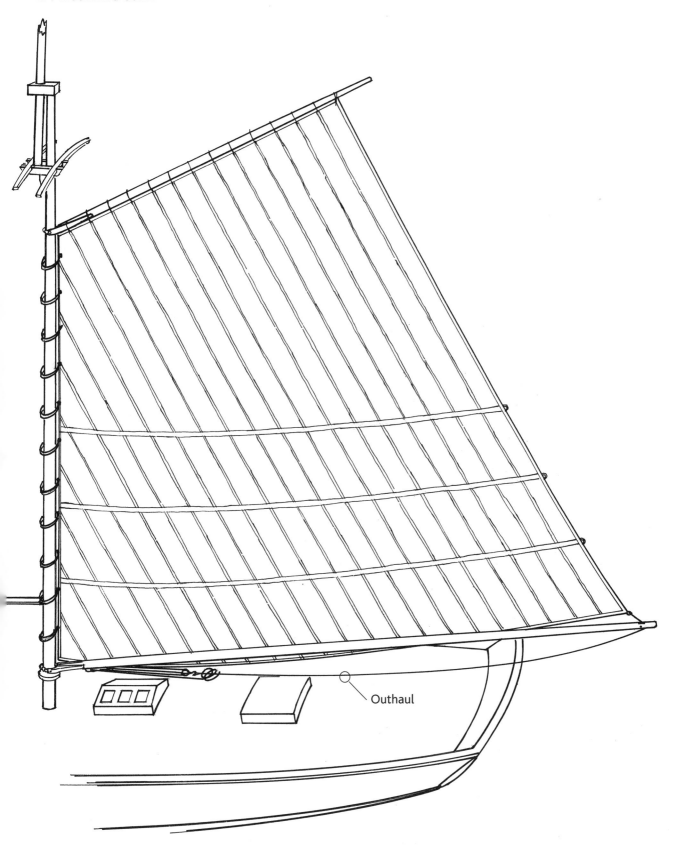

Outhaul